The Power of
**Physical
Intelligence**

The Power of
Physical
Intelligence

Tony Buzan

Thorsons
An Imprint of HarperCollins*Publishers*
77–85 Fulham Palace Road
Hammersmith, London W6 8JB

The website address is: www.thorsonselement.com

 thorsons™

and *Thorsons* are registered trademarks of
HarperCollins*Publishers* Ltd

First published 2003

10 9 8 7 6 5 4 3 2 1

© Tony Buzan 2003

Tony Buzan asserts the moral right to be
identified as the author of this work

Mind Maps® is a registered trademark of The Buzan Group
Original Mind Map concept © Tony Buzan

Plate section illustrations by Emily Burton
Text illustrations by Emily Burton and PCA Creative

A catalogue record for this book
is available from the British Library

ISBN 0 00 714789 9

Printed and bound in Great Britain by
Martins The Printers Ltd, Berwick upon Tweed

dedication

The Power of Physical Intelligence is dedicated to my martial arts
Senseis who taught me that Physical Intelligence is as much about
<u>mental</u> strength and power as it is about physical strength and power:
Tatsuo Suzuki 8th Dan (Karate); Minoru Kanetsuka 6th Dan (Aikido);
John Bush Renshi 6th Dan Kyudo (Japanese Archery); 3rd Dan (Kendo);
3rd Dan Eido (Sword Art); 1st Dan Shotokan (Karate); Michael Gelb
3rd Dan (Aikido); and Kurt Bartoli 5th Dan (Aikido), who kindly
awarded me my 1st Dan (black belt) in Aikido.

contents

list of Mind Maps®

Summary Mind Map® of Motivation.

Summary Mind Map® of Chapter 1 – based on the strengths and weaknesses checklist.

Summary Mind Map® of Chapter 2 – exercises for relaxation and de-stressing, such as yoga, Alexander Technique, Pilates, swimming, running and meditation.

Summary Mind Map® of Chapter 3 – exercises for energy.

Summary Mind Map® of Chapter 4 – vitamins.

Summary Mind Map® of Chapter 4 – diet.

Summary Mind Map® of the Chapter 5 – the Body's Major systems, starting with the Brain at the centre.

Summary Mind Map® of the components that make up Physical Intelligence and how to visualize and divide up the day.

physical intelligence stars

Christopher Reeve

Michael Schumacher

Venus and Serena Williams

Paula Radcliffe

Ian Thorpe

Tiger Woods

Lance Armstrong

Sir Ranulph Fiennes

Sir Mick Jagger

Ellen MacArthur

acknowledgements

Thanks again to my 'Power' Team for this, the fifth book in the bestselling Intelligence Power series. To my Commissioning Editors, Carole Tonkinson and Jacqueline Burns; my Editor, Matthew Cory; my artists and illustrators, Alan and Emily Burton; my designer, Jacqui Caulton; Belinda Budge; Paul Redhead; and Liz Dawson. Thank you once again for standing 'on the shoulders of giants' – your own!

Thanks also to my personal team, especially my Publications Manager, Caroline Shott; my External Editor, Vanda North and her ongoing commitment to global Mental Literacy; my Personal Assistant and dear friend, Lesley Bias; to my dear Mum, Jean Buzan, the best proofreader I have ever met!; and to Dr. Andrew Strigner FRSM, for his dedication and care in training me, for the last 20 years, in the art and science of Physical Intelligence.

chapter one

'Look to your health; and if you have it, praise God, and value it after a good conscience; for health is the second blessing that we mortals are capable of; a blessing that money cannot buy.'

Izaak Walton, *The Compleat Angler*

- Do you often feel tired and lethargic?
- Do you feel you could get more out of life?
- Would you like to be as fit as others you see around you?
- Do you wish you could recapture the boundless energy you had when you were a child?
- Would you like to be more on top of things?

- Have you ever been called a couch potato?
- Do you keep putting off exercising although you know it is important?
- Do you long to look in the mirror and feel good (*really* good!) about yourself?
- Are you confused about your diet because of all the contradictory information you receive?
- Do you get every cold, sniffle and flu bug that is going around?
- Do you only think of your physical fitness when you are sick or ill?
- Have you ever experienced the guilt trip of paying for membership in a health club and then beating yourself up because you keep putting off going – so losing money as well as staying unfit?!

the ppi promise

The Power of Physical Intelligence will put the zip and zest back into your life, help you become fit, and help you get back on top of things (and your life!). This book will show you the right exercises for increasing your strength and energy, teach you what to eat for a healthy diet, and supply you with information about yourself that will amaze you.

what is physical intelligence?

Physical Intelligence is your ability to understand, love and nurture your body, and to have it function at maximum efficiency for you.

When you are Physically Intelligent you will understand the relationship between your brain and your body, and the truth in the saying '*mens sana in corpore sano* – healthy mind–healthy body, healthy body–healthy mind'. This is the new study of **Holanthropy**, so you are about to become an **Holanthropist**!

why does physical intelligence matter?

Does it matter to you that:

- Your body can fight off invaders?
- Your muscles can do the tasks you need them to perform?
- Your skeleton is resistant to breaking?
- Your senses are operating maximally?
- Your energy levels are high?
- You look attractive and radiant?
- Your stamina is superb?
- Your body and mind are relaxed?
- You stay fit happy and healthy throughout your life?

This is why Physical Intelligence is important! The rest of this book is devoted to what matters ...

how will the power of physical intelligence help me?

Firstly, this book will benefit you by helping you to realize that no matter what kind of shape you are in at the moment – and no matter what age you are – you can improve all aspects of your physical health.

The Power of Physical Intelligence is your introductory operations/instruction manual on how to look after yourself. It has been designed like a pocketbook or palm pilot which you can carry around with you for instant and easy reference when you are training, when you want to know about the nutritional value of certain foods, or when you need information on your physical body and its needs. While on the fascinating journey on which you are about to embark, you will:

- Learn how you can control your amazing body with your amazing brain.
- Discover basic exercises for building your muscular power and strength.
- Acquire the formula for creating your own healthy diet.
- Create for yourself a new perspective on drugs.
- Identify your body's major systems.
- Learn the secrets of poise, grace and elegance.
- Discover that you are protected by the galactic-sized armies of your immune system!

- Explore ways of improving your health and quality of life with age.
- Make 'friends' of the great Physical Intelligence Stars.

In addition, *The Power of Physical Intelligence* has been designed to stimulate you, challenge you, and help you have fun as you become healthier, happier and fitter, and take control of your body and life.

physical intelligence - strengths and weaknesses

To help you assess your current state of Physical Intelligence, take a few minutes to fill in the following Physical Intelligence Questionnaire. Give yourself a rating of excellent, good, average, poor or disaster (!) for each component of your Physical Intelligence.

Give yourself:

10 points for excellent
8 for good
6 for average
4 for poor
2 for disaster.

	Excellent	Good	Average	Poor	Disaster
Mental self-control			✓		
Energy levels			✓		
Poise/elegance			✓		
Strength			✓		
Physical flexibility			✓		
Physical stamina/aerobic fitness			✓		
Positive attitude	✓				
Body knowledge			✓		
Knowledge of Physical Intelligence stars			✓		
Healthy diet	✓				
Knowledge of vitamins and the foods that contain them		✓			
Knowledge of the body's systems and their function and maintenance			✓		
Knowledge of the immune system and its function and maintenance				✓	
Knowledge of the positive aspects of ageing				✓	
Knowledge of the other Multiple Intelligences and their application to Physical Intelligence				✓	

20   8   54   12

Your Score

30–60   You did well to lift up your pen and this book to take the test!
Most areas of your physical and mental health would benefit
from *The Power of Physical Intelligence*. Concentrate on
every area of your weakness and develop it into a strength.

60–90   This score puts you in the low to average range. Some
aspects of your health are good, others weak. Use your
strengths to bolster your weaknesses and, as your first goal,
aim for a well-balanced Physical Intelligence.

60–120   An average to good score. You are well on your way to
becoming Physically Intelligent! Make a particular note of the
areas in your questionnaire which are your weakest, and use
the Power of Physical Intelligence to start strengthening them.

120–150   You are an all-round healthy individual! Use *The Power of
Physical Intelligence* to fine-tune your health, expand your
basic knowledge, and learn from the Physical Intelligence
Stars. You will soon be joining them!

FROM STRENGTH TO STRENGTH
a physical intelligence tale

By the time I was in my mid-20s I had become what I thought was physically fit. I had gone from being the traditional 'seven-stone weakling' to being a swimmer, runner, budding karate exponent, weightlifter and physical fitness coach.

I thought I had arrived!

Not so – as I was soon to find out!

At the time I had a friend, Kurt, who did similar activities, and who was also an accomplished horseman, all-round athlete and stuntman. We had heard about the 'new' Japanese martial art of aikido, so one evening we went to a beginner's class to find out what it was all about. A motley group of about 14 individuals shuffled nervously on the side of the dojo, waiting for the class to begin. Our instructor, a five-foot Japanese 5th Dan, dressed in the traditional black 'skirt' of the Samurai warrior, strolled up and down in front of us, examining us all intently.

Finally, he came up to Kurt and me and said, 'Haawww, you two look velly fit, velly strong!' and he beckoned us onto the mat with a flick of his head. We both thought how perceptive he was to recognize the superb state of our physical fitness. How little did we know ...

The Sensei walked into the middle of the mat, and knelt down, his shins resting on the mat, his buttocks resting on his heels and his body perfectly relaxed and poised.

He calmly held out both his arms so that they were straight, parallel to the mat, and extended them directly to his left and to his right. He then gestured that Kurt and I should stand on either side of him.

'Glab lists!' he said, 'making me fall over!'

Kurt and I looked at each other in disbelief. Did he really want two powerhouses like us to make a fool of him in front of a beginner's class? Surely there could be nothing easier than pulling a small man off balance when two much bigger men had two hands on each of his wrists?

As the Sensei continued to kneel and look forward, Kurt and I nodded to each other and indicated: 'Backwards.'

We simultaneously grabbed his wrists ... and simultaneously experienced the first of a number of shocks that were about to happen in rapid succession. His wrists, rather than feeling like a small man's wrists, felt like a fire hose with the water turned full on!

Unsettled, we nevertheless carried on, and together gave an enormous yank to topple him (easily, we thought) backwards.

The second shock – he didn't fall backwards! Instead, his fire-hose arms moved slightly backwards and then returned to their original position. The truth was beginning to dawn ...

Turning to us he said, 'Haawww, must glip lists harder!' and so we did. Kurt and I communicating by eye and slight head nods, tried surprising him backwards again, then sideways, and finally forwards.

The same thing happened – nothing! With a wry grin on his face, the Sensei said, 'Must glip harder: must tly harder!' and *still* nothing happened.

Eventually, as Kurt and I continued our futile efforts, the Sensei said 'Haawww – not so stlong! Not so powerful!' and as he said this, he gently gestured with his wrists and hands.

The result of this minor movement was that both Kurt and I ended up in crumpled heaps on the floor beside him, as the watching beginners – and, eventually, us as well – all laughed.

The lesson the Sensei had taught was a profound one. Physical Intelligence and power is not just muscular strength and general fitness. In addition to these necessary qualities, it is the *mental power and fitness* that can direct the otherwise physically fit body to even greater feats of strength, power and 'intelligence'.

It is for this reason that *The Power of Physical Intelligence* focuses on these mental aspects, giving you a complete operations manual for developing both your body and mind in harmony so that each may gain maximum benefit from the other.

an overview of *The Power of Physical Intelligence*

The Power of Physical Intelligence is divided into 10 chapters, each one dealing with a specific aspect of your Physical Intelligence, building to an integrated whole by the time you reach Chapter 10.

In this opening chapter you have already discovered the definitions and benefits of Physical Intelligence and the new science of Holanthropy, of which you are now an enthusiastic student!

The amazing martial arts story has set the theme of *healthy mind–healthy body, healthy body–healthy mind*. The remainder of this chapter will give you a clear picture of the delights awaiting you in each of the subsequent chapters, as well as outlining some of the special features of *The Power of Physical Intelligence* which will add to your entertainment, learning and enjoyment.

CHAPTER 2: Mind Over Matter

In this chapter you will learn more about the mind–body connection, starting with a brief adventure into the past to discover that all the great civilizations came to the same conclusion – that your Physical Intelligence is fuelled by your brain. This will be illustrated by an amusing story of a young recruit undergoing his first training in the army.

You will meet the first of your 10 Physical Intelligence Stars – Superman! His real-life story is more remarkable than anything ever told in the comic books or movies.

You will learn how you are more powerful than you think, and how you can become more powerful simply *by* thinking. You will also learn about the art of positive thinking and will solve the dilemma of why the negative thinker is usually more 'right' than the positive one – and is therefore actually more wrong! In relation to this, you will meet your second Physical Intelligence Star and discover why Michael Schumacher *is* the world's greatest Formula One driver.

CHAPTER 3: Exercises for Energy

To be Physically Intelligent you must be physically fit and strong.

Chapter 3 introduces you to a full range of exercises for building the kind of body you wish to have, while at the same time showing you how to minimize the risk of injury.

There are further illustrations of the incredible power your mind has over your body as well as the extraordinary potential your body has to change and develop. You will also start your personal life plan for increasing your energy and power.

And did you ever wonder about the secret of the Williams sisters' phenomenal rise to pre-eminence in tennis? You are about to find out!

CHAPTER 4: DVD – Diet, Vitamins and Drugs

The avalanche of contradictory dietary information pouring off the presses is not only confusing – it is depressing. Every time you think you've just worked out the ideal diet, along comes another opinion.

In this chapter you will become a dietary Sherlock Holmes. You will learn how to decide what your body needs and what it does not, and how to make intelligent decisions based on many different streams of objective evidence.

Part of your Sherlockian formula will be a complete understanding of what vitamins really are, which you need, and why.

Similarly, I will give you a new perspective on drugs that will enable you to understand them, fear them less, and take control of your relationship with them.

And finally, how *did* Paula Radcliffe suddenly become a world-beater? Read on and find out the answer.

CHAPTER 5: All Systems Go!

Your body is a miraculous integration of 10 master systems that make you the miracle you are. Chapter 5 will give you an insider's guided tour of your magical self with advice on how to achieve 'all systems go'.

And what better Physical Intelligence Star to have in this chapter than the Thorpedo – Ian Thorpe?!

CHAPTER 6: Walk Tall

We human beings evolved to stand fully upright, not fully slouched! There are very good reasons why this is so, and why the design of our skeletal and muscular systems is so incredibly refined.

In this chapter, I will teach you the secrets of balance, elegance and poise, as well as introducing you to ways in which you can improve your physical (and mental) flexibility.

You will meet Physical Intelligence Star Tiger Woods, who is a master of this and other aspects of Physical Intelligence. There are reasons why he is easily the most dominant golfer in the world, and those reasons are *not* that it is simply 'in his genes'. Find out the *real* reasons ...

CHAPTER 7: Protection Force – The 'I' Team

You don't ever need to feel alone! You have an army of friends and fighters protecting you that is greater than all the fighters and soldiers in all the armies throughout human history. You are their leader/commander/empress/emperor. The way in which you lead them determines their co-ordination, strength and ultimate ability to defend you against the raiders from the universe!

These defenders constitute your immune system – the 'I' Team. Read on and learn how to lead them well.

One of the greatest examples of this is Physical Intelligence Star Lance Armstrong, ex-cancer-sufferer and four-times winner of the Tour de France cycling race. You will learn much from him.

CHAPTER 8: Physical Presence – Endurance and Stamina

If all your other systems are working satisfactorily, yet you have no stamina or staying power, you will be missing the vital ingredient of Physical Intelligence and success – persistence. The ability to persist is a hallmark of accomplishment and success, and depends very much on the way in which you look after and train your heart.

Chapter 8 will focus on this, as well as the mental aspects of stamina. Your Physical Intelligence Star here is Ranulph Fiennes, the arctic explorer who has accomplished 'impossible' feats of endurance.

CHAPTER 9: Ages of Man

Are you worried about becoming less physically fit and physically intelligent as you get older? Don't be! Here I will introduce you to remarkable findings about the possibility of living a healthy and very physically active life, well into your second century.

Interestingly, and for reasons of which you will increasingly become aware, performers and conductors naturally have many of the correct formulas in place. Sir Mick Jagger will give you satisfaction in this area!

CHAPTER 10: Physical Plus – Applying Your Physical Intelligence to Multiplying Your Other Multiple Intelligences

Your social, personal, spatial, sensual and creative intelligences are all intimately linked with your Physical Intelligence. Use them all in a direct and harmonious way and each multiplies the power of the other.

Round-the-world yachtswoman, Ellen MacArthur, is a superb example of integrated multiple intelligences.

features

The Power of Physical Intelligence is liberally sprinkled with special features to help you with your progress in understanding and developing yourself:

Physical Intelligence Stars

In each chapter, at least one Physical Intelligence Star is featured, with stories explaining the many factors that have contributed to their success. As you read these stories, underline or highlight the key words or phrases that you think are the most important factors in the development of their Physical Intelligence. As you progress through the book you will find that there are common themes. Note and highlight these, for they will represent a formula for the development of your own Physical Intelligence. In the same way that you will become a dietary Sherlock Holmes, you will also become a Physical Intelligence Formula Sherlock Holmes! If you find them occurring more than once, keep a check of how many times they occur in the characteristics of the Physical Intelligence Stars.

Quotations

The Power of Physical Intelligence is liberally sprinkled with quotations that summarize and crystallize ideas that are important in the development of your body and brain. Many of these come from the Physical Intelligence Stars. Underline or highlight the key words from these quotes and add them to your Sherlock Holmes Formula.

Brain Boosters

Brain boosters are sayings, statements or affirmations that will allow you to use your new knowledge of your Physical Intelligence to imprint metapositive thoughts in your brain, thus dramatically increasing the growth of your body intelligence.

Studies

To help you back up your own activities and self-development programmes, I have included supporting scientific research throughout the text. This will also help you in your Sherlock Holmesian pursuits!

Self-checks and Games

These include quizzes, self-check questionnaires and games. They will allow you to check your current levels of awareness, knowledge and skills – thereby enabling you to improve all three.

Mind Maps

Mind Maps are a thinking tool I developed to help unleash the natural memory and creative thinking capabilities of our human brains. Mind Maps are, literally, the written reflections on paper of the way our brains think internally. They combine the power of your traditional verbal and numerical IQs with your creative IQ to provide you with a thinking tool of extraordinary power.

As linear, monochrome (and boring) notes were to the Industrial Age, so Mind Maps are to the Information Age in which you now live.

In *The Power of Physical Intelligence* you will find Mind Maps that summarize, in an organized and easily understandable way, the Chapters and features of the book.

Using linear notes to develop your multiple intelligences is like giving an astronaut a broomstick and saying, 'There's your equipment – fly to the moon! Mind Maps are your fully-equipped spaceship!

Brain boosters

1 *I am in the process of becoming more Physically Intelligent.*

mind over matter

chapter two

'Our bodies why do we forbear?
They're ours, though they're not we, we are
the intelligences, they the sphere.'

John Donne, *Songs and Sonnets*: 'The Extasy'

'They know enough who know how to learn.'

Henry Brooks Adams

'He who has health has hope; and he who has hope has everything.'

Arabian proverb

---

mind over matter

'They conquer who believe they can.'

Virgil

'Strength does not come from physical capacity. It comes from indomitable will.'

Mahatma Gandhi

'Hewitt spends a lot of time on court thinking, and the clarity of his thoughts is an inspiration.'

Boris Becker – on Wimbledon Champion and World No. 1, Lleyton Hewitt

'You can feel it across the net; you can feel his energy; feel his desire.'

Younes Aynaoui – Wimbledon finalist describing playing the Champion, Lleyton Hewitt

'My Dad always told me: dream big and dream always.'

Barry Zito, US baseball's American League Ci Young Award for 'Best Pitcher of the Year, 2002'

the power of physical intelligence

Think About It

The more you think about it, the more you will realize that your mind is the fundamental master of your body, and that the best relationship for each is when the two operate in complete co-operation and harmony.

Nearly every movement you make, from lying down, to sitting, standing, walking, moving things, to making yourself a drink or a meal is an example of your mind making a decision and your body helping your mind to accomplish your goal.

From these simple illustrations, we realized at the beginning of the 21st century ('The Century of the Brain'!) that there can be much more to it than this, and that your mind can accomplish the most extraordinary things, both for and with the help of your body.

To start with, here is an amusing story told by my good friend Brian Lee about his first and life-attitude changing experience as a young military recruit. Over to you Brian:

'Oh, and by the way ...'

The story is very simply that one arrives at this training establishment. There is a very nasty sergeant, who says with a sneer, 'Welcome to training camp. What we're now going to do is, we're just going to go for a little run, and what I want you guys to do is to get changed into PT shorts and army boots. Oh, and by the way, I'd like you to carry your small packs. Oh, and by the way, I'd like you to put in the small packs the following items ...' – all of which stuffs it absolutely full and it becomes quite a weight. 'And I want you to do that within 10 minutes and I want you to join me here in 10 minutes time and we'll go off for a little run around the tank tracks.'

Now, the tank tracks at Aldershot are training grounds specifically for tanks to go over bumps. They are hillocks probably 20 or 30 feet high – and there are loads of them. But we had to *run* around them with weighted packs! The idea was that you run around this track and you get back totally exhausted, and the guy then says, 'The object of the exercise in running that couple of miles with all that gear on was to test that you are reasonably fit and I'm sure you are very glad that you were able to do that.'

And everybody breathes huge sighs of relief and says, 'Yes, we are all very glad.' 'Well,' he said, 'I tell you what, just to show how fit you *really* are, we're going to do it again.' No one says anything, because you don't say anything in situations like that – you either faint, die or get on with it. And we got on with it. And so around we went again, feeling completely knackered, and we came back some three quarters of an hour later by which time everybody was *completely* shattered. All leaning against one another to stand upright. The guy says, 'There you are! You had absolutely *no* idea what you were *really* capable of. I'm sure you're all amazed. What you've demonstrated is that you could do at least *twice* as much as you did before, which was more than you thought you could do before you started! And here you are, perfectly OK. Do you all agree?' And everybody muttered, 'Yes, true, we are here and we've done it twice and we didn't think we were going to do it *once*.'

'Well,' he said, "I tell you what, just before we go and have tea, we'll do half of it again.' And everybody thought he was joking, but he wasn't joking at all. He took us over a slightly different route where we did half of the course again, and we got back absolutely and completely beyond knackered. But he said, 'Now look guys, when we went back for the third time, it's a very simple message really. *That whatever you think you can do, you can do one hell of a lot more.* Now a hell of a lot more to some people is half as much again. A hell of a lot more to other people is 10% more, a hell of a lot more to other people is 10 times as much as they've already done. What we've done is at least to do 2½ times more than you thought you could. That's an increase of 250%. And for most of you it was an increase of over 300%. Perfectly possible. You've demonstrated it's possible without a great deal of preparation. That is what you can do for yourself. Let's go and have some tea.'

It was as simple as that. It was later on that it began to dawn on me what the real message was. The idea is very simple: that we human beings are capable of huge amounts more than we believe we are capable of because until somebody comes along and pushes us onto a higher level we are working at half cock.

Mind over Muscle

We now know that thinking can have a major impact on our performance. Can it actually affect the physical structure of our muscles?

Yes! As the following study shows.

The Thinking Person's Exercise Programme

In a ground-breaking study, Dr Guang Yue, an exercise physiologist at the Cleveland Clinic Foundation in Ohio, has demonstrated that you can build bigger muscles just by *thinking* about using them.

In a study he presented to the Society of Neuroscience, he showed what happens when 30 young adults spent 15 minutes a day thinking about exercising their muscles. By visualizing the exercise of the little finger, they were able to increase its strength by 35%. Similarly, by thinking about the muscles around the elbow, they were able to improve their performance by 13%.

In the context of these experiments, it is important to realize that all muscle movement is in response to impulses from nearby nerves called motor neurones. The firing of those neurones depends in turn on the strength of electrical impulses. From where? Your brain!

'That suggests that you can increase muscle strength solely by sending a larger signal to motor neurones from the brain,' says Dr Yue.

Having established that thinking changed muscle power in small muscles, Dr Yue and his colleagues decided to go for a larger and more significant muscle – the bicep. They asked 10 volunteers aged between 20 and 35 to imagine, in five training sessions a week, flexing one of the biceps as hard as they possibly could. While the volunteers flexed their muscles, the researchers recorded the electrical brain activity during the session. To guarantee that the volunteers weren't *actually* tensing their muscles, the researchers also monitored electrical impulses at the motor neurones of the bicep. Every two weeks, they measured the strength of the volunteers' muscles.

The amazing result? Not only did they show a 13.5% increase in muscle strength after a few weeks, *they maintained that gain for three months after the training had stopped!*

Dr Yue's research is supported by a growing number of studies around the world, including many on how to improve all forms of sporting performance.

The Great Civilizations Knew it Too!

Our modern scientific findings about the mind and the body are confirming what the great civilizations also came to realize: that brain is superior to brawn. The ultimately intelligent Japanese warrior, the Samurai sword-fighter, had to train to achieve a prodigious intellect, and as well as mastering the martial arts he also had to master the arts of poetry and art. Musashi's *Book of Five Rings* was devoted to explaining how the art of *thinking* created the great warrior.

Similarly, Chinese warriors were taught both fighting and cultural arts, and the most intelligent were rewarded.

Both the Greeks and Romans trained their armies and leaders under the banner of *mens sana in corpore sano*, meaning 'healthy mind–healthy body, healthy body–healthy mind'. In Homer's famous *Iliad*, the great heroes of Physical Intelligence are always dominant because of the power of their *minds*. All the 12 labours of Hercules required 'Herculean' strength of both body *and* mind. In his battle with the giant hydra, it was his brilliant idea of cauterizing her wounds, so stopping the continuing growth of new fighting limbs, that enabled him to defeat her.

Similarly, Odysseus also won his famous victories by thinking. When trapped with a flock of sheep in the cave of the giant one-eyed Cyclops, rather than letting his soldiers eat the sheep in order to survive, he tied his soldiers underneath their bellies so that the Cyclops would not be able to detect them when they escaped from the cave.

The great leaders of more recent times, including Wellington and Napoleon, were also renowned for their emphasis on physical strength and stamina *in conjunction with* the development of prodigious mental strengths and skills.

Think Better – Be a Better Swinger!

In a study conducted by Dr Dave Smith of Chester College and Dr Paul Holmes of Manchester University, volunteers went on a mind/body training programme that improved their golf putting skills *by more than 50% after only six weeks!*

In the study, groups practised different forms of mental training. The methods were as follows:

1 Watching a video of themselves and imagining their own excellent performance.
2 Listening to an audio tape of themselves playing, with an

emphasis on the sound of their putts being holed.

3 Reading a script of their movements, thoughts and feelings while mentally making a putt.

4 Reading a biography of Jack Nicklaus, one of the world's all-time great golfers, for 10 minutes daily.

The results consistently supported 'Mind over Matter', and were amazing:

Type of Practice	Percentage Improvement
Reading Jack Nicklaus	18%
Reading script while mentally making a putt	30%
Listening to tape of holing putts	47%
Watching video and visualizing	57%

Before the study began, Dr Smith and Dr Holmes had 40 golfers, with an average handicap of just over 3, do twice weekly putting practice. The researchers measured the results of the number of putts holed after 15 attempts at three metres (9 feet 9 inches) and the distance the ball finished from the hole if the putt were missed.

Some of these golfers then graduated to the mental training, while the others continued with their normal training. Before receiving the training, the golfers demonstrated similar putting accuracy. After the training, the ability of those using mental imagery increased significantly. They holed more putts, and when they missed, they missed by smaller margins.

The researchers followed those who carried on using the video or tape technique after the experiment, and found that some months later they had significantly reduced their golfing handicap.

Dr Holmes confirmed that the technique works by strengthening the mental pathways involved in making a putt, and therefore strengthening the body's ability to perform that putt.

To understand what this means, simply visualize walking through a cornfield. The first time you walk through it (your first visualization training) you leave a faint pathway. The second time you walk through (your second mental training session) you leave a slightly stronger pathway. The more times you walk through, the stronger and more defined that pathway becomes.

It is the same with your mental pathways. This is one of the main aspects of your amazing mind controlling matter. As Dr Holmes confirms: 'This is a form of virtual reality training that can involve either just your focused imagination or it can be aided by using your club and ball at the same time.'

Dr Smith quoted Jack Nicklaus as further supporting evidence: 'Nicklaus always said he first imagined where the shot would go – and then it would go there!'

One of the most remarkable true-life stories of 'mind over matter' was still taking place as the first edition of *The Power of Physical Intelligence* was being printed. It involves Superman.

Superman – Supermind over Body

Imagine that you are one of the most perfect physical specimens in the world, and that you have developed your body into such a healthy and magnificent state that you are chosen above all the other best bodies to take on the role of Superman. Imagine that you become world famous and continue to hone your amazing body, becoming skilled in many different athletic pursuits, including horse riding.

Imagine then that at the age of 42, at the peak of your physical powers, you are thrown from your horse in a freak accident and land on your head, crushing your spine's upper vertebrae, blocking virtually all neural communication between your brain and your body, and leaving you totally paralysed from the neck down.

Imagine that you are then told that from that moment on you will never walk or move a limb again. From absolute physical paradise to absolute physical hell in one second! What would you do?

Read on and find out what one man did do – and is still doing. The ultimate story of 'mind over matter'.

Physical Intelligence Star – Christopher Reeve

The superhuman of this story is Christopher Reeve, who was chosen to fill the role of Superman (little did they realize how brilliantly they had chosen!) in the early *Superman* films of the 1970s. Rather than sinking into a slough of despair, Reeve sent out a clarion call of 'mind over matter'. He told the world that he was going to walk again; he told this to all those in similar positions to re-establish their hope and to follow him out of their wheelchairs; and he told his medical team to use every possible avenue and every iota of power in *their* amazing brains to make sure that he *and they* accomplished the impossible goal – and that in the process he would make them as world famous as himself.

Christopher fell from his horse in 1995. His injuries were horrific. 'It's the absolute nightmare of all spinal cord injuries,' said Andrew Casden, Associate Director of the Spine Institute at Beth Israel Medical Centre in New York. 'We generally don't see improvement in these patients.' For five unrewarding years Christopher saw virtually no improvement. He was so paralysed that he could only breathe with the help of a ventilator and had to rely on the power of his mind to keep him alive and to prevent all his systems from collapsing.

In 1999, the Mind and Body Team of Christopher and Dr John McDonald, a neurological surgeon at Washington University in St Louis Missouri developed a new routine. Three times a week, electrodes were attached to Christopher's legs, while he sat strapped to a special exercise bicycle, using visualization techniques of the type described earlier. Electrical currents made his leg muscles rhythmically contract, working the bicycle for an hour per day, and thus exercising Christopher's cardiovascular system as well as his muscles and his visualizing mind.

In separate sessions, Christopher worked on other parts of his body, including his abdominals, triceps, biceps, deltoids and wrists (*see* Chapter 3). The muscles inevitably strengthened. As they did, Christopher began a series of exercises in a pool, where he gradually gained the ability to push off from the edge and to take small steps while being held upright in the buoyant environment. He *said* he would walk again, and the first steps had already been made!

The goal of all the mental and physical exercise was to gain strength, improve circulation and build up his cardio-respiratory endurance. Equally important was to build the neural pathways (the routes through the cornfield) to educate mentally and physically the few surviving spinal nerve cells, teaching them to make new connections and take over tasks that the severed nerves used to do.

By November 2000, Christopher had finally gained control of some muscles – the muscles of his index finger. Other fingers followed, and then the right hand came under his control. Next he got his arm and leg muscles moving. Christopher could now lift his right hand off the table by bending his wrist, and move his arms and legs while lying down.

In addition, his sensory perception improved even more! By July 2001, he could feel the touch of a finger on his skin over about half of his body, and more recently has been able to detect pinpricks, heat and cold.

Staggeringly, where he used to score a 12 on a sensory scale of 0–100, he now scores *close to 70!*

Equally amazing, using a medical scale on which 'A' is total paralysis and 'E' is normal, Christopher went from an 'A' three years ago to a 'C'. This is the first documented 'two-letter improvement' in *any* patient more than two years after an injury.

In addition to all this, Christopher is now regularly off the respirator, and can propel himself through water. His mind and body therapy has increased his muscle mass, reversed his bone-weakening osteoporosis, and reduced the frequency of infections, thereby dramatically boosting his quality of life.

Christopher's doctors report that, taken together, the improvement exceeds anything previously documented in the medical literature with someone with an injury as serious as Christopher's. 'If you'd asked me two years ago if he'd be able to move even his hand today, I'd have said, "No,"' said Dr John Jane, the University of Virginia neurosurgeon who first operated on Christopher after the accident.

In Christopher's typical positive and future-thinking fashion, he said, 'I feel that the progress I have made so far is symbolic of the progress that is yet to come.'

As a result of Christopher's efforts, 500 paraplegics at academic research centres in the United States, Europe and Japan are hanging from harnesses, walking on treadmills and attaching themselves to robots designed to help them move their paralysed arms, legs and bodies. Many who had limited sensations in their lower bodies can now walk for short distances, unassisted or using walkers.

His ultimate goal now? Still the same – full recovery. Where once virtually everyone, including the senior members of the medical profession were saying there was no hope, now everyone is cheering him on: one of the most remarkable cases of 'mind over matter' in medical history.

Superman – Supermind.

Michelangelos of the Mind – Visualize it; Sculpt it; Become it!

The incredible power of 'mind over matter' demonstrated by the experiments and by Christopher Reeve, surrounds us in everyday life – it is the bodies of all those other human beings we see, including ourselves.

All human beings start out as babies who are quite similar in shape. The form we evolve into as adults is a result of the form of exercise that we do (or don't!), the diet we eat, and the general way in which we look after our bodies. Apart from very minor genetic variations, illness or environmental disaster, *the choice of how our body is shaped is a matter for our minds.*

In a very real sense you are the Michelangelo of your mind, and *The Power of Physical Intelligence* is designed to help you sculpt the masterpiece you wish, whether it be a David or a Davidia!

Similarly, many children, especially when examinations are approaching, can use the power of their minds to 'sculpt for themselves' nosebleeds, change their body temperatures, change their blood pressures, and produce vomiting, spasms and any number of skin rashes. In each instance, it seems that once again the upper brain is controlling the lower in order to produce the desired result.

Positive/Negative; Right/Wrong

How can it be that the negative thinker is more 'right', the positive thinker more 'wrong', yet the positive thinker 'wins the battle'?!

Studies have shown that when asked to predict their future, negative thinkers are generally more accurate than positive thinkers. These results are used by negative thinkers to confirm that they are the real 'realists' and that the positive thinkers are wrong-headed idealists. It sounds convincing, but (as you would expect!) there is a fatal flaw in the negative thinkers' argument.

All that the negative thinker has to do to be more accurate, is to predict that things in relation to him/her will not happen – and then guarantee that the prediction is accurate by doing nothing to *make* such things happen. The positive thinker, on the other hand, is by definition a risk-taker, who predicts that things will change, and then sets about trying to bring about such change. Some 'failures' are bound to happen, and therefore the positive thinkers' percentage accuracy slips below the perfect non-action score of the negative thinker.

However, looked at in another light, the positive thinker is *far* ahead of the negative.

- **How many positive changes does the negative thinker bring about? None!**
- **How many positive changes does the positive thinker bring about? Many!**

The negative is more 'right'; the positive is more 'wrong'; yet the positive really wins hands (and brain cells!) down!

This sentiment is admirably summed up by Wayne Gretzky, the greatest ever ice-hockey player who said,

'You miss 100% of the shots you don't take.'

You are about to meet your second Physical Intelligence Star – Michael Schumacher. Now that you are far more aware of the incredible power of the mind over the body, you will appreciate even more Michael's story and his rapid rise to prominence in the world of Formula One racing. As you read, or after you have finished reading, remember to underline or highlight the key mental attributes that you now think have helped make Michael the great World Champion that he is. When you have identified them, begin to apply them to your own life.

Physical Intelligence Star – Michael Schumacher

Michael Schumacher, the five times Formula One Champion is an ideal example of 'Mind over Matter': the matter of his body, and the matter of his Formula One Ferrari …

When he was still only 33 years old, *The Times* enthusiastically proclaimed:

> 'The welter of statistics he has piled up in the past dozen years are extraordinary, so extraordinary that even his biggest critics are finding it difficult to deny him his place in the pantheon (of genius). He has overtaken both Ayrton Senna and Alain Prost for victories and challenged Sir Jackie Stewart and Jim Clark for their tenacity and skill.'

Michael was born on 3 January, 1969 near Cologne in Germany, and was the son of a builder. While a little boy, he became passionately interested in go-carting, spending much of his time racing, and he rose to the top of the junior ranks. Did this interfere with his schoolwork? On the contrary, it helped him to focus even *more*. Like most Physical Intelligence stars, Michael is well-rounded and practises healthy mind–healthy body. At school he excelled in Maths and English, as well as Soccer and Judo – a well-balanced mind and body combination that he was to apply to his racing career.

Michael is particularly famous for his mental focus, which he displayed immediately after leaving school. Rather than going for a high-paying professional job which he could have easily acquired, he went to work in a garage as a mechanic.

Why? Because he wanted to learn *everything* about his life-vision of being the best driver in the world. With total focus and determination, he worked his way up to Formula One, where he began to compile those '*so* extraordinary' statistics:

- German Junior Go-Cart Champion: aged 15 years
- German & European Senior Go-Cart Champion: aged 17 years
- Career fastest laps: 51 (next best, Alain Prost: 41)
- Grand Prix starts: 170
- Front row of grid: 78
- Top three: 111 (a staggering 65% of races entered)
- Wins to race ratio: 2.88 (the highest of any driver in history)
- Wins: 64 (the highest of any driver in history; next best, Alain Prost: 51) ¬and still extending further away from his rivals
- Points in a season: 144 in 2002 (set previous record with 123 in 2001)

the power of physical intelligence

- Wins in a season: 11 (next best, himself – 9!)
- Widest championship winning point margin: 67 in 2002 (beat previous best of 58 *he* set the previous year!)
- Consecutive races in points: 22 (previous best, 15 by Carlos Reutemann, 1980–1)
- Schumacher has had a podium finish in his last 19 consecutive races, including every race in the 2002 season – another first!
- World Championships: 5 (tied with Juan Fangio for the most ever)
- To emphasize the fact that he is getting better with time, in 2002 Michael raced to that fifth World Championship more rapidly than anyone else in history

In addition to these scintillating performances, Michael has exhibited incredible consistency and reliability, coming in the top six in 167 of his 172 races! Furthermore, Michael has done what few other champions could do, and that is to win in all weathers, rain, wind, cold or hot, and on all forms of tracks, both fast and slow – his versatility knows no limits. During this time, Michael has become renowned for his positive 'can do' attitude of overcoming any problem with which he is faced.

So was all this due to simply having the best cars and luck? On the contrary, it was entirely due to a prodigious amount of work and to Michael's mental ability to *create* 'luck'. His first two Championships were with the unfancied Benneton team, after which he moved to what was then a shambolic Ferrari team where he immediately assumed complete responsibility and leadership, and for six years he focused on building an outstanding, perhaps the best, Formula One racing team in history.

As Jeff Gordon, four-times champion of America's NASCAR racing circuit says of Michael,

'Not only does he have the ability to make the car go fast, but he seems to have the ability to be a leader. His determination shines through to everybody around him. It seems he's just as hungry as any one person can be, and so the whole team rallies around that.'

The Technical Director of Ferrari, Ross Brawn explains how Michael uses his extraordinary creativity to create his own 'luck':

'Michael is able to cope with mechanical adversity better than any driver I know. There are various things that might stop you finishing races – braking or engine problems for instance – but Michael is able to adapt his driving to keep the car going.'

Brawn found out about Schumacher's mastery of the improbable in the 1994 Spanish Grand Prix at Barcelona when his car jammed in fifth gear on the 24th of 65 laps.

'Over the radio we told him to press on because we thought he might just be able to scrape the odd point that would help his World Championship bid. But he adapted his driving style completely and was actually taking some corners faster in fifth gear than he had been taking them earlier when he was technically in a more suitable gear. Michael went on to finish second. It was a remarkable drive.'

So is it luck? No, it is Michael's mental ability to control himself and his machine as Brawn concludes, 'He is so adept at handling the key elements of the job that he makes the odds work in his favour.'

As *The Times* sums it up:

'A driver who can win on every type of circuit in any conditions and against any opponent, who can lead his team from the front and who can command a huge volume of technical detail required of the modern Grand Prix driver, demands our attention.

'This weekend, Silverstone will be privileged to see a genius at work. They come along rarely in any sport: in motor racing Fangio was the first but Schumacher is the latest and, arguably, the greatest.'

Michael's Mind over Michael's Matter!

physical intelligence workout

1 Decide on the body form you ideally wish, and begin working on your own 'Michelangelo Sculpture'. Use this and the forthcoming chapters in *The Power of Physical Intelligence* to help you accomplish your goal.

2 Search for more stories such as that of Christopher Reeve, and build up an imaginary 'Mastermind Group' with whom you can have virtual conversations concerning what they would recommend to you in terms of developing your own Physical Intelligence. You will be amazed at some of the stories you discover and some of the advice you receive!

3 Review the Physical Intelligence 'key concepts' you have identified from this chapter before starting the next.

4 Select one of the following Boosters, and take a few seconds three or four times a day, especially when you are in a quiet place, to repeat it to yourself 10 times.

Brain boosters

1 *My mind is helping to improve the health of my body.*
2 *My mind is helping to sculpt the shape of my body.*
3 *I accept 'failure' as an opportunity to learn and improve.*
4 *I am constantly improving my body talk.*
5 *I am an Holanthropist!*
6 Mens sana in corpore sano *is my motto for life.*
7 *I am a healthy thinker.*

chapter three

'Better to hunt in fields, for health unbought,
than fee the doctor for a nauseous draught.
The wise, for cure, on exercise depend;
God never made his work, for man to mend.'

John Dryden, Epistle: 'To my honoured kinsman John Driden'

'Concentration is the secret of strength.'

Ralph Waldo Emerson

This chapter is devoted to helping you develop your muscular power
and strength. In doing so you will streamline and sculpt your muscles,
increase your overall energy levels, strengthen your bones and make

them more flexible, increase your ability to pull, push and lift, protect yourself against injury, strengthen your immune system, and considerably improve your self-confidence.

These exercises, combined with a healthy diet and good poise and flexibility (*see* Chapters 4, 6 and 8) will help you get into the best shape of your life!

In this chapter I am going to introduce you to an overall musculo-skeletal workout that will help you develop and improve the health of the muscles in your neck, shoulders, arms, back, chest, stomach, upper legs and lower legs – in other words, all the major muscle groups of your body.

Happily, the muscle groups of men and women are virtually identical, so the exercises described are equally beneficial to both sexes. Only a few years ago, weight training for women was considered inappropriate, and destined to produce 'unsightly muscles'.

Fortunately, the tide of opinion has now changed and, as Libby Purves recently observed in *The Times*:

'Gradually, in recent years, muscularity has become an intriguingly desirable ingredient of feminine beauty.'

The centuries-old assumption that women are both weak and physically ineffectual has now been laid to rest. Indeed, in many sports women are not only catching up with the male of the species, they are overtaking him! (*See* Chapter 8.)

It is only in recent times that the unexercised female body has been

the power of physical intelligence

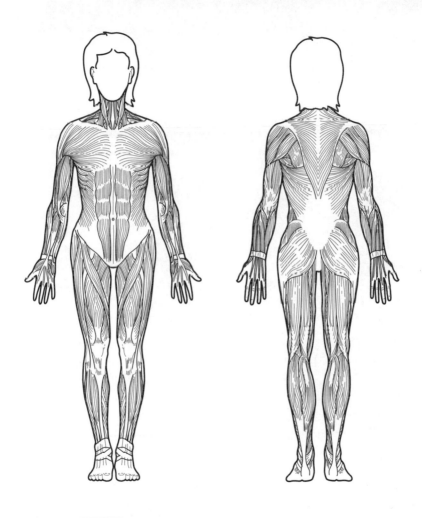

exercises for energy

considered 'sexy'. In most societies it was the well-exercised female who was considered the most seductive.

In all animal species, the natural and desired state for the female is robust health.

Lisa Lyon, the pioneer in the field of women's body building, and renowned as one of the most beautiful and attractive people in the world, said that training had transformed her from feeling like a sloth to feeling like a panther.

This is the ideal goal for the female human.

For both sexes, a healthy, streamlined and strong body is the *natural state*, and is something the entire world is rapidly coming to realize, as the following three vignettes tell.

Even Presidents Do It

Where once politicians, like golfers, were considered to be portly and not particularly fit, the trend is now rapidly changing, and from the top.

The Russian President, Vladimir Putin, is a practising black belt in judo, and as well as this he still engages in sambo wrestling, skiing and long aerobic walks. As a result of his involvement in physical exercise, and his obvious awareness of the benefits it brings him personally, professionally and in terms of his renowned energy and stamina, he has opened a nationwide campaign to get the entire Russian population back into the gym. Putin is introducing exercise programmes in offices and factories, and asking every town and village in the country to promote a healthy lifestyle and to become involved in national sports competitions. He wants a 'culture of healthy lifestyle' to pervade Russia.

On the 'opposite side', President Bush, who is a known exercise practitioner, recently completed a 4.8 kilometre run in 20 minutes 30 seconds, and has been pronounced in top shape as a result of his ongoing exercise regime. President Bush, who is 55, lifts weights in the gymnasium, runs a good few kilometres at least four times a week. He talks publicly about how the time he invests in his exercise and health pays dividends in his overall energy levels, his ability to combat stress and his ability to deal with the arduous travel and other commitments of the Presidency.

Like President Putin, President Bush wants all Americans to follow his example. He recently stated that if he, the President, could find time to exercise, then so could most other people, and they should! After his most recent fitness test, the President was considered in the top two per cent of fitness of men his age – a more than competitive level for veteran competition.

Like Presidents Putin and Bush, Prime Minister Tony Blair also pays close attention to his health, monitoring his diet and taking regular exercise. Blair takes fish oil supplements every morning, and considers exercise so important to his regime that he has installed a rowing machine at Downing Street on which he regularly works out.

What is true for Presidents is also true for kids.

FACT: A British Medical Association Survey reveals that 33% of English children are overweight, of whom 10% are obese.

The Government Centers for Disease Control and Prevention in America confirm that about 40% of American children are now overweight, 11% being obese. It is thought that this is partly caused by the fact that the average American child spends four hours a day sitting in front of a television or computer screen.

Recent research on the benefits of exercise has also laid to rest the myth about bright kids being weak, spindly nerds. All the studies report exactly the opposite.

FACT: Between the ages of 10 and 16, the amount of after-school exercise declines steadily with every passing year. By the age of 16, girls are exercising 200% less.

In England, a project called 'Fit to Succeed', in which 11-year old children from seven different middle schools were encouraged to take part in regular physical exercise and training, demonstrated the link between academic performance and physical exercise.

The highest scores in the government SAT (Standard Assessment Task) tests have consistently been scored by the children who exercised at least three times a week. The study showed, for example, that more than 60% of the 11-year old boys who achieved Level 5 in their maths SATs – above average for the age group – had taken part in hard exercise the previous week on at least three occasions. Steve Kibble, a senior physical education advisor, commented:

> 'More active children are more alert. After exercise the metabolism is raised for four or five hours, a fact supported by medical evidence … Physical activity … does help maximize learning potential.'

The same proved true in many other studies around the world.

FACT: **Exercise rises with education. The percentage of people who engage in 'vigorous' leisure-time activities for at least 20 minutes, three or more times a week, buy educational attainment.**

Degree	Vigorous exercise percentage
Masters/Doctorate	33.7%
Bachelors Degree	30.8%
Associative Arts	23.1%
High school graduate	14%
Some High school or less	7.9%

In a French study, children had their normal timetable modified. Academic instruction was curtailed by 26% and was limited to mornings. The afternoons were occupied by a wide range of physical activities such as gymnastics, swimming and sport. Regular rest periods were also included.

The fascinating finding was that although the extra-activity group was getting 26% less time in the classroom, their marks were identical to those taking much more academic instruction and no physical education. The 'physically active' group were also more calm and attentive, and seemed to enjoy *all* activities more.

In another French study, children who were given extra daily physical activity by a specialist, once again taken from lesson time, actually outperformed children getting less physical activity.

These results were duplicated in an Australian study by an Adelaide student group who were given more fitness activities. Two years later, the 'extra-active' children had higher arithmetic and reading scores, as well as better all-round behaviour. As Ben Tan, Director of the British Heart Foundation's National Centre for Physical Activity and Health at Loughborough University, who has reviewed much research, said:

'There does seem to be a strong correlation between high levels of physical activity and high academic achievement in schools. It increases the concentration of children and their ability to learn. In schools that invest in physical education and after school sport you can see a major improvement in academic achievement.'

the power of physical intelligence

In England, Stephen Smith, Chairman of the Headmasters' and Headmistresses' Conference Sports Sub-Committee, and head of Bedford Modern School says:

'There is plenty of evidence that sport is linked to the development of the whole person. It's to do with discipline, targets, health, and can improve academic performance.'

His views are boosted by research on the 100-plus sports colleges recently set up in England. Far from being academic wastelands, sports colleges are, according to Tessa Jowell, Secretary of State for Culture, Media and Sport, 'seeing academic performance improve faster than in any other type of specialist college.' Unpublished DFES (Department for Education and Skills) statistics reveal that the rate of improvement is twice that of a standard comprehensive school. 'It is powerful evidence that if you link sport with the curriculum, exam results go up,' says Jowell.

All these researches are further confirmed by the Qualifications and Curriculum Authority who, after extensive research, conclude that frequent participation in physical activity enables young people to improve their physical competence, confidence and levels of attainment, health, fitness, well-being, self-esteem, motivation and, crucially, their attitudes to, and engagement in, learning.

Why are these results so consistent? Because increased physical activity increases blood flow to the brain, and when coupled with learning tasks (physical or mental) causes the formation of dendrites –

slender filaments that branch out of the neurones and increase the neural pathways and neural mapping of your brain. It is these multiple physical interconnections that increase intelligence in mammals and foster greater learning through improved intelligence. As Dr Susan Greenfield, Professor of Pharmacology at Oxford University says:

> 'The brain is very sensitive to what is happening to the body, and the more you are interacting and stimulating the circuits of the brain, the more agile are your brain cells.'

Agile brain cells, agile body; agile body, agile brain cells!

It works for the bodies and minds of Presidents and kids. It will work for yours.

Preparing for Your Body/Mind Workout

Before getting down to the actual business of exercising, let's first dispel a couple of false beliefs about exercising.

False belief: 'Never drink water while exercising – you don't need it till after.'
Truth: Your body is composed of 90% plus water and your muscles of more than 70% water – you need a lot. When you are exercising, your body cells need your arteries in particular to be adequately supplied with fresh water so that the system can transport the nutrients including vitamins, minerals and carbohydrates, to your working muscle. At the same time, they can also get rid of their waste products.

If you become at all dehydrated, your whole system gets 'clogged up' and everything you do requires more strenuous and inappropriate effort. Drink roughly a pint (½ litre) of water for every half-an-hour of reasonable exercise.

Drink regularly throughout the day, (6 pints/3½ litres of liquid is a good average) except at meal times, when water tends to unnecessarily dilute the digestive juices, putting added strain on your stomach and intestines.

False belief: 'Use salt tablets to prevent cramps and fatigue.'
Truth: You do need salt, but certainly not in tablet form. When you are exercising strenuously, you will perspire, and in the process lose salt. This needs to be replaced.

Taking a salt tablet, however, is both brutal to your body and counterproductive. Salt in this form is used to dry out meats, and the lump of solid brine represented by a salt tablet will do the same to the delicate mucous membranes of your stomach. This can cause extreme discomfort, nausea and vomiting.

To replace salt, take a little extra with liquid or fruit before exercising, and a little extra after your exercise. Make sure that all you are doing is replenishing the supplies you have lost.

False belief: 'Extra protein makes you strong.'
Truth: Protein makes you strong. Extra does not. In a study at the Harvard Fatigue Laboratory, which was designed to indicate the body's protein requirements, subjects were fed a regular diet which was totally devoid of protein.

They all remained normally healthy for three weeks, only beginning to show signs of protein deficiency after one month. This experiment confirmed that the body has ample supplies of protein, and if you take in a regular, varied and healthy diet, no protein supplementation is necessary (*see* Chapter 4).

False belief: You only have one muscle that pumps blood around your body – your heart.
Truth: You have millions! Each of your muscle fibres acts as a 'mini heart' as it expands and contracts during movement and exercise helping to pump blood to all your body systems. The more fit, strong, great in number and flexible they are, the more capably can they pump greater volumes of fresh oxygen to your body, and especially, to your brain.

The Meta-Positive Exercise Habit

In 1990, as part of the Allied Dunbar National Fitness Survey, more than 4,000 adults were questioned by researchers on their behaviour, attitudes and beliefs about activity and fitness.

The results were disturbing! Only 2% of those who were inactive when young were active as adults. On the positive side, 25% of those who said that they were active as teenagers continued to be active as adults.

the power of physical intelligence

As you prepare to go into your first full Power of Physical Intelligence Energizer Workout, here is a little story to amuse you:

Arnold Schwarzenegger, when asked why he carried on bodybuilding and weight-training when it was so boringly repetitious, replied that on the contrary, it was one of the most stimulating and exciting pursuits possible. He explained that at full intensity, the emotions and feelings he and others experienced were almost akin to sexual orgasm.

When criticized for being narcissistic, he responded that just as Michelangelo had sculpted marble into the form of his vision, he, Arnold, was doing the same thing, only using different sculpting materials: the components of the human body!

'Muscle Pack' Energizer Exercises

These exercises that follow are designed to give your musculo-skeletal system a complete and healthy workout. You will begin to reap the benefits of these exercises right from the start. Here are a few pointers to make sure you derive maximum benefit:

1   Start with weights that are far lighter than you can handle. This is to allow your body to become used to the new exercises, to allow you to develop efficient technique without strain, and to allow your muscles to adapt to the new routine without injury.
2   Do each exercise 3 times, with a minute rest in between. In each exercise repeat it 5 or 6 times if you wish to build large muscle bulk; 10–12 times if you want leaner, more stamina-filled muscles.

3 When your muscles are becoming properly conditioned (probably from between exercise session 6 to session 10) you can graduate to 'maximum weight'. This means the weight that you can comfortably lift for the first set of repetitions, becomes a good effort by the end of the second set of repetitions, and that you can only just manage at the end of the third set of repetitions. At this weight your body will get the message that it needs more muscle-power to handle the task it is being asked to do. It will automatically build extra muscle for you!

4 Ideally, exercise in front of a mirror, so that you can adjust your poise and perfect your technique as you exercise.

5 To engage your brain further in your physical activity, repeat your selected Brain Boosters as you exercise.

For convenience and efficiency, these exercises have been designed to allow you to perform with the minimum of equipment: either with simple dumbbells, standard weight-training equipment, or just yourself!

Edwin Moses, one of the greatest athletes and 400-metre hurdlers ever, who went undefeated in over 80 national, international, world championship and Olympic events, said that he considered push-ups to be one of the best all-round muscular body toning exercises.

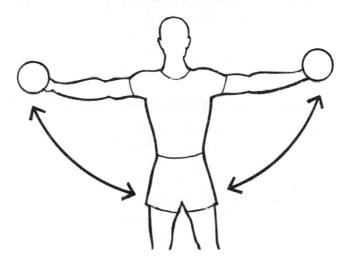

Shoulders – Side raises

1 Stand upright with your feet approximately shoulder-width apart; your hands freely extended by your sides; your poise excellent. Each hand will hold a dumbbell, your palms facing in to your thigh.

2 As you exhale, lift the dumbbells out until your arms are parallel with the ground. Do this to the count of one. Hold them for a count of one. Lower them to a count of two.

Remember: to breathe evenly and deeply, exhaling when exerting effort, to maintain your poise.

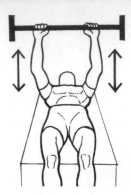

Chest – Barbell Bench press

1　Lie down on the bench, your feet slightly more than shoulder-width apart. Place yourself under the barbell so that it is directly over your chest. Your grip should be even on the bar, each hand just beyond shoulder width.

2　First lift the weight off its holdings, and lock your arms straight. Then slowly, to a count of two, lower the bar to the nipple area of your chest. Hold for a count of one.

3　Drive up for a count of one. Hold again for a count of one with your arms locked, and then repeat.

Remember: keep the rhythm smooth and steady. Bouncing the weight off your chest loses you the benefit of the exercise.

Keep your back in contact with the bench throughout. Breathe in during the hold periods; breathe out while exerting effort.

If you can't find any equipment for this exercise, push-ups are also an excellent method for toning up and building the chest muscles.

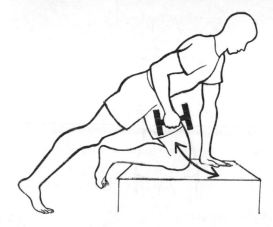

Back – One-arm dumbbell rows

1   In this exercise one knee rests on a low bench, the other foot is resting comfortably on the floor. You are in a 'half-kneeling' position. One hand should be just in front of you on the bench, the other holding a dumbbell parallel to your extended leg. Make sure that your back is straight throughout the exercise.

2   To a count of one, pull the weight up, so that your elbow is as far up as it can go. The dumbbell will end up next to your chest. Hold for a count of one and then lower for a count of two.

3   When you have completed reps with the 'first arm' perform exactly the same exercise with the other.

Remember: throughout the exercise allow your neck to be free and your back to lengthen and widen. As usual, inhale during pauses; exhale during effort.

Arms (Biceps) – Dumbbell curl

1   Stand as you did for your shoulder dumbbell raises.
2   Taking advantage of the spiral nature of your musculature, with
    your palms facing forwards, raise the dumbbells to shoulder
    height, allowing your palms to turn outward as you raise the
    weight.
3   Keep your upper arms and torso still throughout the exercise,
    and focus on your biceps. Maintain your upright posture –
    swinging back and forward can lead to injury. Count one for the
    lift, one for the hold and two for the 'let down'.

This exercise can be done by lifting both weights simultaneously, or by
lifting them one after another in a 'walking' motion.

Remember: Poise is paramount in this exercise – make sure you keep
your head, neck and spine aligned.

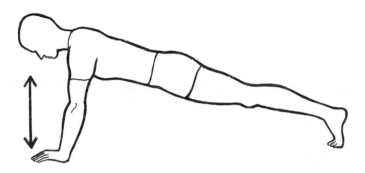

Arms (Biceps) – Push-ups

Push-ups are also an excellent exercise for the triceps, and require no extra equipment. When doing them it is important to make sure that your counting is slow and extended, because it is your body weight that is the 'resistance' with which your muscles are exercising.

You can increase the intensity of this exercise, first by extending your raising and lowering time; second by increasing the distance of the exercise by raising yourself on your fists rather than your palms; and third by placing your feet on a chair, bench or any other raised surface to increase the weight that is placed on your arms.

Remember: keep your body poised and straight throughout this exercise. When you 'touch down' in the standard push-up, make sure that the whole of your front touches the ground simultaneously. 'Bum in the air' lessens the effect of this exercise!

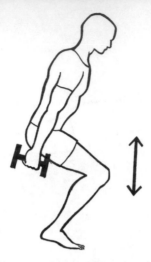

Thighs (Quadriceps: front) – Dumbbell squats

1 As with your shoulders and biceps exercises, stand with excellent poise, a dumbbell in each hand.
2 While maintaining your poise, bend at the hips, knees and ankles until your thighs are parallel with the floor.
3 Hold for a count of one, and then, pushing from your heels, raise yourself to your starting position, maintaining poise throughout.

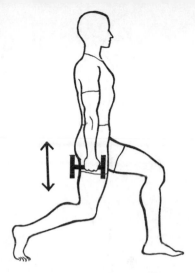

Thighs (Hamstrings: back) – Dumbbell lunges

1 Start in exactly the same position as for your dumbbell squats. Step gracefully forward with one foot, bending at your knees and lowering your hips until your front leg has its thigh roughly parallel with the floor, your hind leg has its knee nearly touching the floor.

2 After a count of one, push off with the leading leg, raising yourself back to the starting position.

3 Complete the reps for one leg first, then transfer to the other.

Remember: your toes should be facing directly to the front throughout the exercise. Keep your front foot flat throughout. Keep the movement smooth, rhythmical and poised.

Lower Leg (Calves) – Dumbbell angled calf raise

1 Stand exactly as with your previous dumbbell exercises. Once in this position, turn both your toes out, so that your feet are each at an angle of 45° (from 'straight ahead'). Keeping your legs straight throughout the exercise, first raise up on your toes as high as you can possibly go to a count of two.

2 As usual, pause for a count of one and then slowly lower to the count of two back to the starting position.

Remember: maintain your poise – excellent balance throughout this exercise gives an even workout to both the left and right calf muscles.

Torso (Abdominals) – Floor crunches

This, like the push-ups, is an exercise in which the only equipment you need is yourself!

1 Lie on the floor, bring your knees up together, with your feet at hip-distance apart flat on the floor. Place your hands beside your head.

2 This exercise actually starts with your back. Start by pushing it into the floor. In this position, roll your head and shoulders up, keeping the rest of you stationary. In this position your stomach muscles are holding your upper torso in place. Hold the position for a count of one, tensing your stomach muscles even more as you do so.

3 Next, slowly lower your head and shoulders back to the floor, continuing throughout to push down with your lower back.

Remember: This is not a speed exercise or a competition to see who can do the most 'sit-ups' as they were once called! The whole advantage of this exercise comes from maintaining the tension on your abdominal muscles and flexing them as hard as you can. Even though this is a 'lying down' exercise, maintain your poise. Scrunching up your chest, neck and throat reduces the effectiveness of the exercise. You want your abdominals to do all the work. Therefore, make sure your hands stay by the side of your head, and do not slip round to the back to support it.

Now that you have a full understanding of physical power of strength and how to develop it, you will appreciate more fully how our next Physical Intelligence Stars used it to help them become dominant in their chosen sport.

Physical Intelligence Stars – the Williams Sisters

How did two little African-American girls, who grew up playing tennis on potholed courts, rise to become the numbers 1 and 2 tennis players in the world?

Answer: Strength, Power, Energy and Attitude.

From an early age the two little girls, Venus and Serena, and their father Richard, shared a vision of becoming the best in the world. They then single-mindedly (or in this case triple-mindedly!) worked towards that goal.

One of the main factors was strength training, a controversial idea at the time, but one that has now been proved to be vital if you are to reach the top in tennis.

The girls have honed themselves to perfection, their bodies being described as machines that can compete with cougar-like prowess and muscular power. This training has brought them to such a level of fitness that Serena recently claimed that she has so much energy that she never gets tired. Reflecting her upbeat and positive attitude, when one writer referred to her big shoulders, she riposted, 'you mean, sexy body!'

The strength training they have committed themselves to has laid the foundation for the development of the other Physical Intelligence skills necessary for world dominance. As Richard Evans in the *Sunday Times* explained:

'... then came the ability to co-ordinate the various movements required to propel the ball back again, low and hard, on the run, for jamming on all the brakes a human body possesses; swivel and hare off in the opposite direction. They were doing this 10, 20 times in a series of volleys that would have left their illustrious predecessors – the Everts, Navratilovas, Goolagongs, maybe even Steffi Graff – sucking air as legs turned to jelly.'

Indeed, the Williams sisters have raised the women's game to new levels of skill and athleticism; some even say to 'heavenly heights'.

Both Venus and Serena are also renowned for their extraordinarily positive mental attitude. They are known as fighters who are able to come back and win from 'lost' positions, and similarly come back from career-threatening injuries. As Venus, who tries everything from acupuncture to massage therapy to keep her fit and well, said about being No. 1: 'I think it's just about an attitude. The kind of attitude you take out there towards your game, towards everything. It pays off.'

Serena also helps dispel another popular misconception: that physical training has to be only 'serious'. The opposite is true: it *has* to be fun. As Greg Boeck, sports special correspondent for the *USA Today*, reports

'Focus on The Laugh. You can't miss it. It defines Serena Williams. It's her calling card, the window into her soul. She has laughed her way to the top of the tennis world with her aggressive game, fun-loving personality, witty demeanour and bold attitude.'

The sisters' mother, Oracene, says, 'The Laugh is Serena's best trait.' Serena agrees. 'I think so, because if you can't laugh yourself out of a situation, then life gets a bit too stressful or you just won't be happy. It's important, whatever you are doing, to be happy. That's why I like to smile and laugh. I enjoy myself.'

Like other great athletes, such as Michael Schumacher, Tiger Woods and Mohammed Ali, the Williams sisters' positive attitude and mental focus often beats opponents before the physical matches actually start. Using your growing knowledge of the mental element of Physical Intelligence, analyse the following statement by Jennifer Capriati, who was comfortably the No. 1 women's player in the world before being dethroned by the two Williams.

'There's a difference between wanting to and then expecting yourself to and thinking that you should be up there (at number one). Of course, a lot of other people should be up there. It's something that I haven't really felt in a while, and maybe I've been feeling it even more lately.

'I don't know, it's just a lot of stuff going on, maybe. Human beings are the only ones that go over and over and do the same mistakes over and over. We never learn. It's still a different kind of pressure, and that's something I have to go back and figure out.'

Unless Jennifer learns the true nature of 'mind over matter', the Williams sisters are in for a long reign with no challenge from her!

Nor indeed can they expect a challenge from another rising star, the French tennis player Amelie Mauresmo. When asked how she intended to challenge the Williams sisters, she replied: 'I can't. I'll have to wait until they drop off a bit. I have the number three spot as my goal right now.' With such thinking, Amelie is dooming herself never to become No. 1.

In addition to their stated philosophy of 'playing your best at all times', Venus and Serena are also known for their powers of concentration and creativity. They prepare for every opponent by working out their strategy in advance, and if they find that this is not working, they immediately and flexibly adapt to the situation.

Serena sums up the mental approach that has allowed them to achieve such high physical accomplishments:

'Normally when you set your goals, you set them above what you can reach. You reach for the sky and land on a star. That's how I normally do it.'

Venus and Serena are wonderful examples of Physical Intelligence at its highest level.

As *The Times* warned the other top women tennis players:

'The rest of the field had better start working on their physiques too.'

Brain boosters

1 *My Physical Intelligence Scores are becoming better and better.*
2 *I look for sources of enjoyment in every physical exercise I do.*
3 *I constantly encourage myself while exercising.*
4 *I look to the 'Stars' in Physical Intelligence for inspiration and guidance.*
5 *I am guiding my body to maximum health.*
6 *After exercise I take appropriate rest.*

The Energizer Exercises with which you are now familiar are made even more beneficial if your muscles are supplied with a superb flow of nutritional energy. Find out how to maximize this in the next chapter.

DVD – diet, vitamins and drugs

chapter four

'I saw few die of hunger; of eating, a hundred thousand.'

Benjamin Franklin

'Always rise from the table with an appetite, and you will never sit down without one.'

William Penn

'All philosophy lies in two words, sustain and abstain.'

Epictetus

DVD – diet, vitamins and drugs

'A well-governed appetite is a great part of liberty.'

Seneca

'When it comes to eating, you can sometimes help yourself more by helping yourself less.'

Richard Armour

'Tell me what you eat and I will tell you what you are.'

Anthelme Brillat-Savarin

what to eat?

Overwhelmed by the tidal waves of dietary information pouring off the presses every week? Confused and frustrated by what appears to be contradictory 'perfect solutions'?

Worry no longer!

In this chapter you are going to become a dietary Sherlock Holmes. I am going to lead you through a series of investigations that will provide you with the clues to solve the 'Case of the Mystery Diet'.

You will be surprised and pleased to discover (as you will!) that there *are* fundamental truths and guidelines to human diet that will enable you to scythe through all the 'fluff' you might read, so you can to make intelligent and objective decisions about what your ideal diet is.

By the end of this chapter *you* will have a broader base and understanding than many dietary 'experts'. *You will be the expert!* You will know what is best for yourself and will be able to plan your own diet with knowledge and confidence.

In the course of your Holmesian investigations, you are going to explore all those areas about which so many alarmist books and articles have been written:

1 Vitamins
2 Calories
3 Fat
4 Ancestral habits
5 Human design
6 What the studies say
7 The balanced diet

You are going to start your investigation by looking at vitamins. You will soon discover why they are so vital to your life, and how simple it is to organize a diet which guarantees that you get a proper supply.

vitamins – what are they, what do they do, what foods contain them?

Vitamins are life-givers and life-sustainers. They are *vital* to your well-being and health. The very word 'vitamin' is based on the Latin *vita* meaning 'life'. This is also the root of the word 'vitality', and so you can clearly see that 'vitamins' are a source of your own 'vitality'. They are a group of organic compounds essential for normal growth and nutrition. What distinguishes them is that they are only required in very small quantities in your diet and, unlike many other products, mostly they cannot be made (synthesized) by your body. You have to acquire them from external nutrition.

As you read about each of the vitamins – and the foods in which you can find them – circle those foods containing each vitamin that you would like to include in your diet, making sure that you ensure an adequate supply of each vitamin. When you have done this you will have designed a diet that is far more nutritious, and that will give you far more vitality, than most of the dietary fads popular at any one time.

The main vitamins, their function, and foods in which you can find them, include the following:

Vitamins
Vitamin A (Retinol)

Function: Main 'ingredient' in your night vision. Protects your immune system, provides nourishment to skin, eyes, hair, nails, the mucous membranes and the adrenal glands. Fights infection, helps you utilize your good fats and enhances the functioning of your thyroid and liver. Involved in repair and growth processes. A stress reducer. Helps clear vision; assists growth and reproduction.

Found In: Nuts, green and yellow vegetables (cabbage, spinach, lettuce, carrots, etc), natural oils, eggs, fish-liver oils, liver.

Vitamin B1 (Thiamin)

Function: Maintains normal carbohydrate metabolism. Maintains nervous system functioning. (*Note:* vitamin B1 is readily lost from your body, so should be replaced daily.) Provides good muscle tone to the cardiovascular system, especially the heart; reduces fatigue, aids digestion, protects immune system

Found In: Brussels sprouts, lettuce, beans, peas, carrots, apples, apricots, bananas, raspberries, grapefruit, hazelnuts, almonds, oats, rice, sweet corn, egg yolk, liver, potatoes, brewer's yeast.

Vitamin B2 (Riboflavin)

Function: Basic ingredient for healthy hair, skin and nails; protects adrenal glands from damage caused by stress; protects immune system. Essential for cell maintenance, especially repair after injury; essential for energy metabolism.

Found In: Lettuce, cress, spinach, nettle leaves, beans, peas, cauliflower, apricots, peaches, plums, pears, almonds, walnuts, peanuts, rye, oats, barley, rice, milk, eggs (especially egg yolk) fish, liver, kidney.

Vitamin B3 (Niacin)

Function: Improves cardiovascular system; essential to your brain metabolism; protects immune system. Involved in most bodily processes, and present in every one of your 60 trillion cells.

Found In: Nuts, soya beans, brewer's yeast, wholegrain cereal, fish, poultry, liver, kidney.

Vitamin B5 (Pantothenic Acid)

Function: Decreases toxicity of many drugs; increases the body's ability to withstand stress; protects against radiation damage to cells; protects immune system. Essential for energy metabolism; essential for the formation of acetylcholine – a substance necessary for proper memory function.

Found In: Wholegrain cereals, legumes, brewer's yeast, eggs, poultry, fish liver and kidneys.

Vitamin B6 (Pyridoxine)

Function: Vital for the production and health of DNA and RNA (your genes!); helps in the formation of collagen and elastin; protects the immune system. Essential for fat, sugar and protein metabolism.

Found In: Beans, peas, potatoes, lettuce, tomatoes, whole grains, brown rice, brewer's yeast, sunflower seeds, hazelnuts, peanuts, bananas, milk, egg yolk, fish, lean muscle meats, liver.

Vitamin B12 (Cyanocobalamin)

Function: Helps keep intestinal flora healthy, therefore aiding digestion; synthesizes nucleic acid; protects the immune system. Important in fatty acid and protein metabolism; essential ingredient in the production of red blood cells.

Found In: Most raw vegetables, whole grains, yeast, wheat germ,

**milk, cheese, oysters, clams, sardines, herring, salmon, liver and
kidneys.**

Vitamin C (Ascorbic Acid)

Function: Major helper in the formation of connective tissue, teeth
and bones; strengthens blood vessel walls; helps wounds heal faster. As
a natural antioxidant, vitamin C helps prevent colds, coronary heart
disease, swollen and painful joints, while counteracting the toxic effects
of drugs. Protects the immune system. Widely involved in almost every
bodily function. (*Note:* vitamin C is water-soluble and easily lost from
the body. It should be replaced daily for optimum health.)

Dr John Brifa reports that higher levels of vitamin C in the body are
associated with improvement in mood and intelligence and a reduction
in everyday errors of memory and attention.

Vitamin C is arguably the most well-known and popular vitamin in the
United Kingdom – £30 million a year is spent on this supplement alone!
**Found In: Brussels sprouts, peppers, curly kale, broccoli, other raw
green vegetables, tomatoes, fresh walnuts, strawberries, oranges,
lemons, grapefruit, rosehips, potatoes, onions, dandelion salad.**

Vitamin D

Function: Essential for the absorption of calcium, and therefore for
the growth and maintenance of healthy bones. Regulates calcium and
phosphate metabolism; messenger and regulator.
**Found In: Sunlight!, most green leaves, cereal germ, yeast, milk,
butter, egg yolks, fish liver oils, tuna, salmon.**

Vitamin E (Tocopherol)

Function: Major force in the development of healthy reproductive functions; essential in protection of mother and child during pregnancy. Natural antioxidant which stimulates skin cell metabolism; protects the immune system. Crucial to normal procreation; widespread actions throughout the body.

Found In: Most green leaf vegetables, vegetable-based fats, wheatgerm oil, soya oil, peanuts, all cereal grains.

Remember Vitamin E!

A study on vitamin E, published in *The Archives of Neurology*, took place from 1993 to 2000, with a follow-up period of three years. The researchers looked at the relationship between vitamin E intake of 2,889 participants – aged 65–102 – and their mental abilities. The findings indicated that those who took the largest amount of vitamin E (about 258 milligrams daily) showed 36% less memory loss than other participants who took the least amount (4.5 milligrams daily).

The researchers concluded: 'Vitamin E intake, from foods or supplements, is associated with less cognitive decline with age.' It does indeed seem that vitamin E can help reduce problems of memory loss and learning caused by unhealthy ageing!

Vitamin F (EFAs)

Function: Vital for your cardiovascular system, as it helps reduce excessive cholesterol, and prevents both heart disease and arteriosclerosis.

the power of physical intelligence

Found In: Most grains and seeds, especially linseed.

Vitamin H (Biotin)

Function: Helps in the synthesis of fatty acids and glucose. Helps maintain healthy skin, protects immune system. Essential for metabolism of carbohydrates and fats.
Found In: Yeast, liver, egg yolk, soya beans, brown rice.

Vitamin K

Function: Essential for coagulating the blood, and therefore a major factor in your defence against injury to your cardiovascular system; important for liver function; provides extra energy to your body's cells.
Found In: Curly kale, green cabbage, spinach, nettle leaves, yoghurt, milk, eggs, fish liver oils.

These are your *essential* vitamins. You need them *all*.

Calories – Your Energy Units

Calories are not, as is often hinted, your enemies. They are your friends!

Firstly, calories are not 'things' as many people think. They are simply a measurement of energy. The good news is that a calorie is a *tiny* unit of energy, and *we don't need many of them to get through a good, healthy, active day*.

To show you just how tiny a unit a calorie is, one calorie is the amount of energy you need to raise the temperature of a few drops of

---

water a mere single degree centigrade – hardly anything at all!

And so, Sherlock, here is the vital information you need: from being totally inactive (lying in bed all day!) to superbly active (Olympic training) you need between 1,500 calories to 5,000 calories per day.

The formula is so easy! First, you decide on the level of activity you wish to maintain (*The Power of Physical Intelligence* recommends a level requiring between 3,000 and 5,000 calories per day). Then put your investigative magnifying glass on the following pages. In them I have included tables of food portions which will provide you with 100 calories so that you can begin to work out your daily portions, as well as some general physical activities and the number of calories that you expend per minute performing these activities.

This will enable you to balance the energy you take in and the energy you put out.

To help you even further, I have included ideal weight tables for normal, healthy and active bodies. These tables will enable you to take in more than you put out if you are underweight; put out more than you take in if you are overweight; or maintain an equilibrium if you are already in the 'good weight' zone.

One additional advantage of being healthy is that in the event that you do binge at any time, your body will be far more resilient to such an 'attack'. It will be able to rebound more rapidly, and to get rid of any excess and poisons more efficiently. Being fit allows you to misbehave with fewer repercussions!

self-check

This table shows how little food you actually need in order to provide your body with its minimum requirement of 1,500 calories per day.

Food portions which provide you with 100 calories:

Amount	Foodstuff	Amount	Foodstuff
1	cup of orange juice	¾ cup	cereal
5	fresh peaches	2 tbsp	sugar
½	cup of rice	1	fried egg
⅓ cup	spaghetti with tomato sauce	5 oz	glass of milk
1¾ cups	strawberries	¼ cup	tinned tuna
15	almonds	½ cup	tomato or vegetable soup
1	big apple	8 oz	glass of soft drink
⅓ cup	baked beans	⅔ oz	chocolate
8 oz	beer	1 oz	whisky
1 oz	Cheddar cheese	2 oz	minced beef
1	grapefruit	1	baked potato
1	honeydew melon	6	crisps
1	lettuce	5	French-fried potatoes
1 cup	coffee with cream and sugar	1¼	apples
1	pancake	1/12 quart	ice cream
		2	plain biscuits

self-check

This table shows the calories expended per minute in standard physical and athletic exercises.

Activity	Calories Expended per Minute
Walking 2 mph	2.8
Walking 3.5 mph	4.8
Bicycling 5.5 mph	3.2
Bicycling rapidly	6.9
Running 5.7 mph	12.0
Running 7.0 mph	14.5
Running 11.4 mph	21.7
Swimming (crawl) 2.2 mph	26.7
Swimming (breaststroke) 2.2 mph	30.8
Swimming (backstroke) 2.2 mph	33.3
Golf	5.0
Tennis	7.1
Table tennis	5.8
Dancing (foxtrot)	5.2

We now know the adage 'You are what you eat' to be true. Eat with intelligence and become more intelligent!

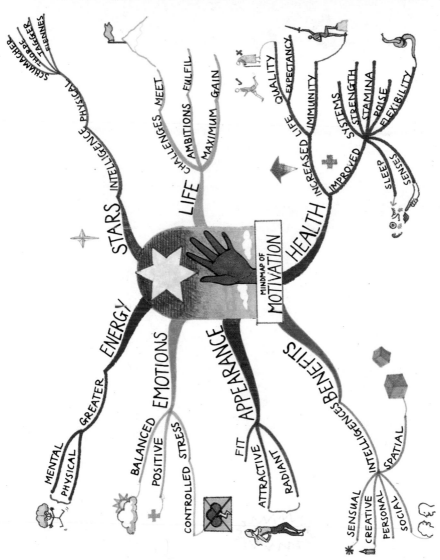

Summary Mind Map® of Motivation

Summary Mind Map® of Chapter 1

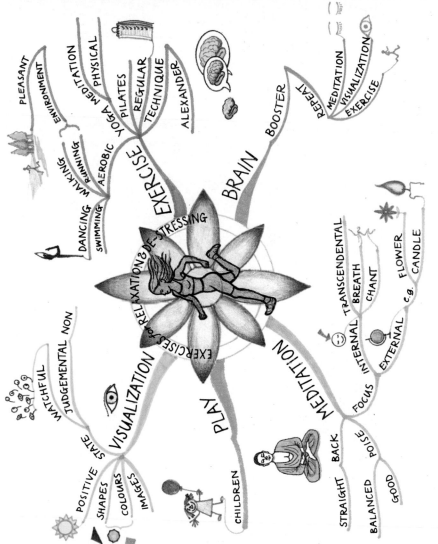

EXERCISES for RELAXATION & DE-STRESSING

EXERCISE

PHYSICAL

MEDITATION
YOGA
PILATES
REGULAR
TECHNIQUE
ALEXANDER

AEROBIC
WALKING
RUNNING
DANCING
SWIMMING
ENVIRONMENT
PLEASANT

BRAIN

BOOSTER
REPEAT
MEDITATION
VISUALIZATION
EXERCISE

MEDITATION

FOCUS
INTERNAL
EXTERNAL
TRANSCENDENTAL
BREATH
CHANT
e.g. FLOWER
CANDLE

POSE
BACK
STRAIGHT
BALANCED
GOOD

PLAY
CHILDREN

VISUALIZATION
WATCHFUL
NON JUDGEMENTAL
POSITIVE STATE
SHAPES
COLOURS
IMAGES

Summary Mind Map® of Chapter 3

EXERCISES for ENERGY

MOVEMENT
- SMOOTH
- POISED
- RHYTHMIC

EXERCISES
- ARMS
  - BICEPS — CURLS — DUMBBELL
  - TRICEPS — PUSHUPS
- TORSO
  - CRUNCHES — FLOOR
  - CHEST — PRESS — BENCH — BARBELL
  - PUSHUPS — REPETITIONS — PLENTY!
  - SHOULDERS — RAISES — SIDE — DUMBBELL
- BACK
  - 1 ARM — DUMBBELL ROWS
  - ANGLED
- LEGS
  - CALVES — RAISE
  - QUADRACEPS — SQUATS
  - HAMSTRINGS — THIGHS — LUNGES — DUMBBELL

TIPS
- BEGINNERS
  - EXPERIENCED
  - REPETITIONS
    - MUSCLE — BULKY — 5 ~ 6
    - LEAN — 10 ~ 12
  - MAXIMUM
  - + 3 — REST — 1 MINUTE — REPEAT
- BRAIN — BOOSTERS — REPEAT
  - LIGHT — WEIGHT — LIFT
- BREATHING
  - EFFORT — EXHALE — INHALE — PAUSES
- TECHNIQUE
  - POISE — CHECK — MIRROR

MUSCLE
- FIBRES
- MINI-HEART = WORKOUT
- GROUPS
  - SHOULDERS
  - CHEST
  - TORSO
  - ARMS
  - BACK
  - LEGS

Summary Mind Map® of Chapter 4

VITAMINS

A — NOURISHES: VISION CLEAR, NIGHT, EYES, NAILS, HAIR, SKIN, GLANDS ADRENAL, MEMBRANES MUCOUS

B1 — METABOLISM CARBOHYDRATE, MAINTAINS MUSCLES HEART, SYSTEM NERVOUS, REDUCES FATIGUE

B2 — SKIN, HAIR, NAILS, BASIS, STRESS ANTI, REPAIR INJURY, METABOLISM ENERGY

B3 — METABOLISM, BRAIN, SYSTEM CARDIOVASCULAR, IMPROVE

B5 — MEMORY, METABOLISM ENERGY, PROTECTS STRESS, DAMAGE DRUGS, RADIATION

B6 — MAKES GENES COLLAGEN, METABOLISM FAT SUGAR PROTEIN

B12 — METABOLISM ACIDS FATTY PROTEIN, PRODUCTION CELLS BLOOD RED, DIGESTION AIDS

C — WALLS VESSEL BLOOD STRENGTHENS, PAINFUL JOINTS PREVENTS, ILLNESS HEALS, WOUNDS

D — ESSENTIAL CELL METABOLISM, ABSORPTION CALCIUM, BONE MAINTENANCE GROWTH

E — REPRODUCTIVE FUNCTIONS, SKIN, PREVENTS DISEASE HEART

F — REDUCES CHOLESTEROL, CARBOHYDRATE METABOLISM, FAT

H — HEALTH SKIN METABOLISM

K — FUNCTION LIVER, PROTECTS CARDIOVASCULAR SYSTEM

ALL — BOOST IMMUNITY

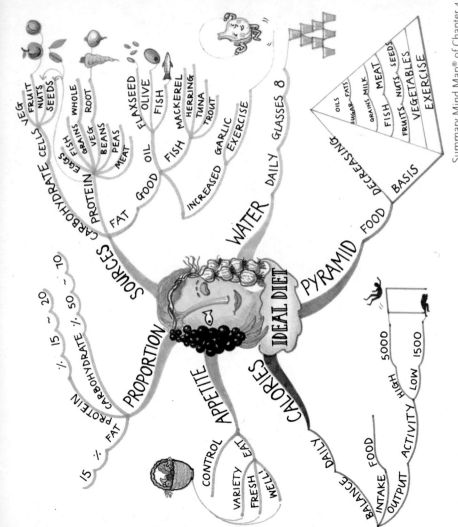

Summary Mind Map® of Chapter 4

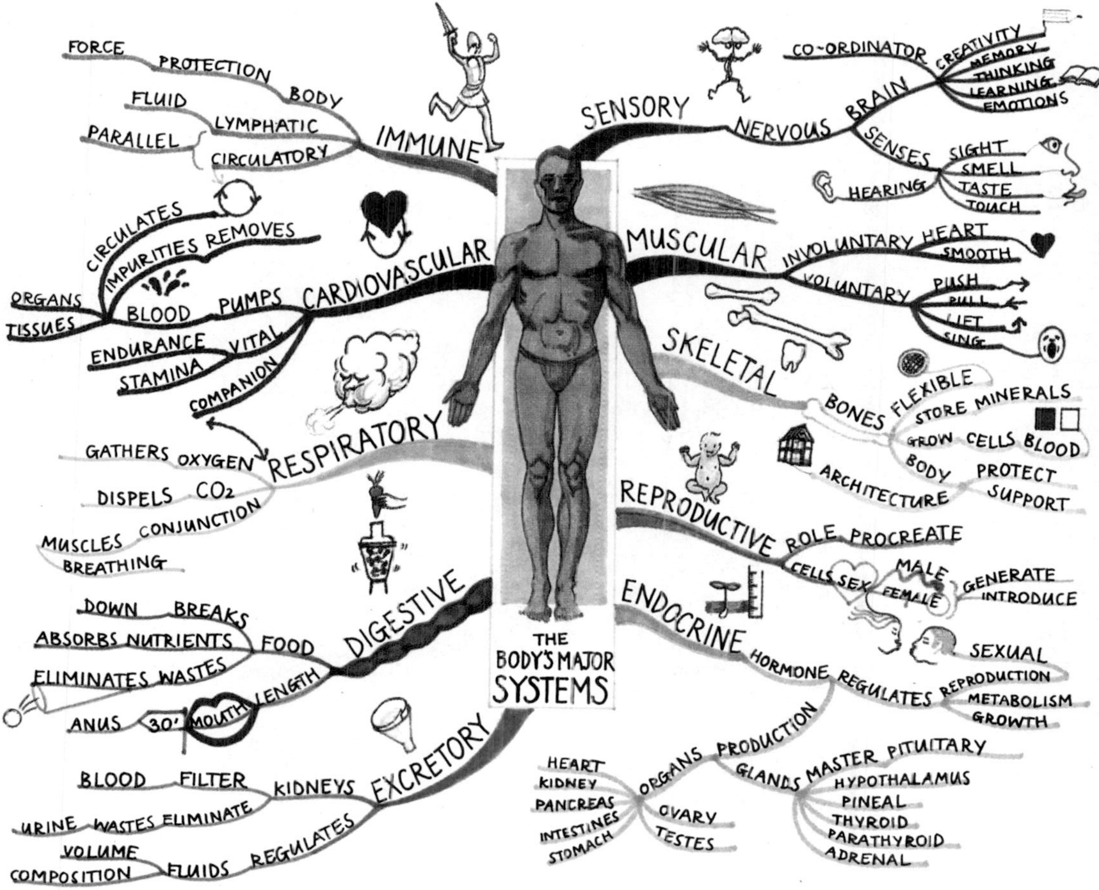

Summary Mind Map® of Chapter 5

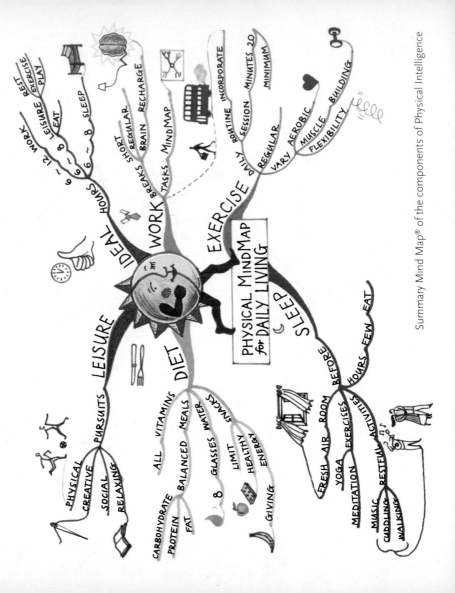

Summary Mind Map® of the components of Physical Intelligence

self-check

FACT: The Health Survey for England indicates that more than 60% of men and 50% of women are overweight. In addition, 21% of women and 18% of men are obese (30 pounds or more over maximum healthy weight).

148 million Americans are overweight. Of these, 44 million are not aware that they are overweight, thinking that they are 'about right'.

Desirable Weights

Men, age 25 and over (weights given in lbs):

Feet	Inches	Small Frame	Medium Frame	Large Frame
5	1	110–118	116–127	126–141
5	2	113–121	119–131	127 142
5	3	116–124	122–134	130–146
5	4	119–127	125–137	133–150
5	5	122 130	128–141	136–154
5	6	126–135	132–145	140–159
5	7	130–139	136–150	145–164
5	8	134–143	140–154	149–168
5	9	138–148	144–158	153–172
5	10	142–152	148–163	157–177
5	11	146–156	152–168	162–182
6	0	150–160	156–173	166–187
6	1	154–165	160–168	171–192
6	2	158–169	165–183	176–197

Women, age 25 and over (weights given in lbs):

Feet	Inches	Small Frame	Medium Frame	Large Frame
4	8	90–96	94–105	102–117
4	9	92–99	96–108	104–120
4	10	94–102	99–111	107–123
4	11	97–105	102–114	110–126
5	0	100–108	105–117	113–129
5	1	103–111	108–120	116–132
5	2	106–114	111–124	120–136
5	3	109–117	114–128	123–140
5	4	112–121	118–133	127–144
5	5	116–125	122–137	131–148
5	6	120–129	126–141	135–152
5	7	124–133	130–145	139–156
5	8	128–138	134–149	143–161
5	9	132–142	138–153	147–156
5	10	136–146	142–157	151–171

To demonstrate even further your body's incredible efficiency, in the course of a fully active 24-hour day in which you include a good weight training session and a good aerobic training session, your body can magically achieve this on the amount of energy it would take to raise the temperature of three bottles of wine by one degree!

Just think of the comparisons:

A standard car's combustion engine operates at an efficiency of 15% and a 'very efficient' diesel engine operates at an efficiency of 30%. Your amazing body operates at 80–100% efficiency!

Now you have a good knowledge of your vitamin and calorie requirements, you are ready to tackle the biggest monster in the menagerie of dietary villains: Fat!

Fat the Monster? Fat the Friend!

FACT: Since the 1950s, the proportion of unnecessary fat in the English diet has risen 50%.

False belief: Fat is bad for you. 'Exterminate! Exterminate! Exterminate!'
Truth: Excess fat is bad for you. Fat is not only good for you, it is so essential that without it you would die!

Now for the *good* news. It is both extraordinary and extraordinarily *good* news.

Researches at the turn of the century by Simon Coppack at the Royal London Medical School, and Steve O'Rahilly, an adipose tissue expert from the University of Cambridge, have revealed that fat sits at the centre of a complex and wide-ranging communications network. The revolutionary discovery they have made is that *your fat is a giant organ*! Not only an organ, but it is now recognized as one of the largest organs of your body. Their discoveries 'made fat much cleverer than it was thought to be before' says O'Rahilly.

Function: What, then, does FAT do for you?

FAT unlike your other organs is spread throughout your body in a number of specialized depots.

FAT is packed around all your internal organs to protect them from trauma.

FAT lines your belly to protect your 'centre' from external damage.

FAT insulates and keeps you warm.

FAT cushions your joints, and increases their ability to repair and maintain themselves.

FAT cushions your heels to protect your spine from jarring impact.

FAT pads out your fingertips to enable you to feel without pain – without fat every touch would be agony.

FAT reduces inflammation.

FAT pads out your eye sockets to keep your eyes and your eye movements 'well oiled'.

FAT is an essential part of your haemoglobin (oxygen carrying constituent of red blood cells).

FAT makes each red blood cell more flexible, thus allowing them to glide more easily into capillaries, thus giving you a better supply of oxygen and nutrients to your tissues, thereby increasing energy.

FAT stores and dynamically 'dishes out' appropriate portions of fat/energy in times of need.

FAT acts as a nutritional buffer, deciding, with the liver and muscles, how to share out your nutritional bounty.

FAT releases extra fuel back into circulation in times of fighting or intense exercising.

FAT is the major source of a set of proteins called 'complement proteins' – the immune system's 'precision bombs'. When released they punch holes in the walls of invading bacteria or diseased cells which your antibodies have marked out for destruction.

FAT supports testosterone levels which, amongst other things, influence and improve muscle strength and metabolism.

FAT actively manufactures the hormone leptin, which briefs your brain on the state of your body's energy reserves.

FAT with water, is the main constituent of the very brain it advises and helps build.

The discoveries reported in the *New Scientist* magazine (16 September 2000) inspired me to write the following summary in a little prose poem:

I am one of the largest
Organs in your body.
A thrifty caretaker,
I carefully husband
Your body's precious reserves,
Resting in the good times
To tide you over the bad.
I influence your behaviour,
Manage your fertility
And shore up your defences
Against microscopic invaders.

Soft and snug
I blanket you
In a warm, intimate embrace,
Cradling your internal organs,
Cushioning your footsteps,
Shielding you from the insults of the world.
I do all this for you.
Don't despise me.
I am
Fat.
Your friend.

So what kind of foods, Sherlock, contain the 'good fats' – the omega-3 fatty acids – which stop your arteries clogging, and which keep other arteries under control?

the power of physical intelligence

Found In: 'Good fat' foods such as:

- **Flax seed oil**
  - **olive oil**
  - **fish oils**
  - **fish, including mackerel, herring, trout, tuna, flat fish and salmon**

Two other 'foods' that increase the level of the 'good fats' in your body are:

- **garlic**
- **exercise**

Your diet is becoming even more rounded (and you less so!) as we move on to the next area of investigation: what your ancestors ate.

The History of Diet – Ancestral Habits

For your next Holmesian investigation, I want you to use your imagination to take yourself back into the world as it was three million or so years ago.

Imagine that you are one of the first humans. You belong to a very small tribe, and have no real tools or weapons. The environment that surrounds you is both natural and wild. You have no preconceptions about what you 'should' and 'shouldn't' eat. And this is the way it will remain for all but the last 10,000 years.

Take yourself in your imagination through a typical day, imagine your activities, and imagine what you would eat. Expand that day into a

---

year – how would the changes in weather, climate and temperature affect your activities, appetite and diet?

You have probably already come to the same conclusion as the anthropologists who have found that the foods our ancestors ate were:
Primarily plants, including leaves, flowers, roots, seeds, berries, fruits and nuts – supplemented by, when and where available, crustacea, fish, grubs, insects, eggs, small animals and birds.

What we did *not* eat, and what our bodies are *not* especially well-adapted for, were:
Grains (too hard and indigestible – as we had not yet discovered the use of fire), milk and its products (we had not domesticated the milk producers), the meat of large animals (they were too dangerous for us to attack without weapons and, conversely, many of them liked to have us as part of their diet!), refined foods (they got everything they needed from the world around them), and additional salts and sugars (again, there was an ample supply in their natural food).

So, Sherlock, do you see patterns developing?

Things will become even more clear after your next investigation:

your body as an 'eating machine'

Again, I want you to use your imagination. This time I want you to imagine that you are the designer of perfect eating machines.

Some of the machines you design are only to capture and eat meat. Some you design to eat only grass. Some you design to eat mostly meat, supplemented by other food; some to eat mostly vegetables, also supplemented by other foods.

Think about how you would design each of the following parts of that eating machine: teeth (front and back); jaw; stomach(s); digestive juices; intestines; and body type, providing power and speed appropriate to the kind of food it needed.

You would have to design what *has* already been designed, wouldn't you?! Your meat eaters would have to have long sharp cutting teeth, stomachs designed to take meat, meat digesting enzymes, relatively short intestines and a powerful speedy body with a strong jaw and large razor sharp teeth in order to capture the meat.

Your purely vegetarian animal would need to have slicing teeth at the front for cutting, and grinding teeth at the back for pulverizing the vegetables, roots and fruits. The stomach or stomachs would need to be comprehensively designed to digest all the different plants, with a longer intestine. The body would need to be stable, and their requirement for explosive speed would not be necessary to hunt a vegetable!

In the light of all this, examine yourself objectively, and decide what you are *designed* to eat. Most people conclude that the foods we are designed to eat are *exactly what our ancestors ate!*

The 'Holmesian Diet' is obviously beginning to take its final form. How do the remaining 'exhibits', the dietary studies and the 'balanced diet', fit in with our developing picture?

Brain Food – What the Studies Say

> **FACT:** In America, about 26% (54 million adults) are obese. This accounts for 300,000 deaths a year, more than Aids and tobacco-related cancers combined.

Vegetables and Fruits

As the arguments raged between carbohydrate-protein and fat-based diets, one researcher saw the way through. Gladys Block of the University of California at Berkeley published, in the last decade of the 20th century, a major review of more than 200 nutritional studies. The results were crystal clear: those who regularly ate substantially more vegetables and fruit than average were up to four times less likely to succumb to a huge range of cancers, including breast, lung and colon. They were also less likely to suffer from heart disease.

The Director of the Rowitt Research Institute in Aberdeen emphasizes how impressive this evidence is:

'This amazing consistency of evidence [over such a wide range of studies makes this] the single most convincing dietary relationship' [known to science].

Vegetables and a healthy heart

A new meta-study, incorporating the findings of the Oxford Vegetarian Study, analysed 28,000 vegetarians and 48,000 non-vegetarians. The findings were significant: over a 10-year period, the vegetarians were 24% less likely than non-vegetarians to die of ischaemic heart disease, including heart attacks.

A further finding was that fish eaters suffer no more heart disease than vegetarians, suggesting that a diet based on vegetables and including fish is a good foundation for nutritional cardiovascular health.

Hooked on Fish

Three new studies show that people who eat oily fish two or more times a week are greatly protected from sudden, unexpected death: an increasingly common condition often caused by severely abnormal heart rhythms.

Study One – 22,071 Doctors

Seventeen years ago Dr Christine Albert, a cardiologist at Brigham and Women's Hospital in Boston, enrolled 22,071 male doctors in a long-term Physicians Health Study. When they enrolled, none had a history of heart disease, stroke or cancer.

During the study, the researchers analysed the blood of 94 doctors who died suddenly of heart disease, and compared the findings with those of 100 surviving members of the study. In particular, they compared the bloodstream concentrations of N-3 fatty acids (Omega-3 fatty acids) found primarily in fish oils.

When the researchers divided all the men into four groups based on the concentration of N-3 fatty acids in their blood, the men in the highest quarter were 80% more likely to survive.

Study Two – Fishwives' Tales

In a second study, Frank Hu and his colleagues at the Harvard School of Public Health, combed through the records of 84,688 women taking part in the Nurses' Health Study. Over a period of 16 years, 1,029 women had heart attacks, and 484 died of heart disease.

Analysis of the nurses' diets showed that the women who ate the most fish 33% less at risk of sudden death, as well as having a moderate reduction in risk of non-fatal heart attack.

Tufts University physician Irwin Rosenberg says Omega-3 fatty acids found in certain fish stabilize heart cells electrically, so that a heart attack won't cause fatal rhythm disturbances. The N-3 fatty acids appear to have a specific anti-arrhythmic effect, possibly by stabilizing membranes of heart muscles cells. The oils also have a blood-thinning effect similar to aspirin.

Although ocean-living, cold-water oily fish such as *salmon*, *swordfish*, *sardines*, *mackerel* and *tuna* offer the largest easily accessible source of Omega-3 fatty acids, there are other sources: *flaxseed oil, canola oil and English walnuts* all contain significant amounts of the oils.

Study Three – Food for Thought

Our brains are dependent on the supply of particular nutrients for their proper functioning. Brain tissue is rich in healthy fats known as PUFAs (long-chain Polyunsaturated Fatty Acids).

A number of studies have found that individuals with lower levels of PUFAs are at an increased risk of mental impairment, such as dementia and Alzheimer's disease. PUFAs are found in abundance in oily fish as mentioned above.

In a Dutch study, men who ate a lot of fish were found to have half the rate of mental decline compared with occasional consumers. Grandma was right – fish *is* a good brain food!

The health study at Brigham and Women's Hospital in Boston, Massachusetts has added further support for fish and fish oil as important constituents in a healthy diet. The study found that the inclusion of fish in the diet cuts a woman's risk of suffering the most common types of stroke. Within reason, the study found, the more fish the better. The study concluded that the Omega-3 fatty acids found in many types of cold-water fish prevent the build up of blood clots which cause ischaemic strokes: those strokes that make up 83% of stroke deaths. Dr Kathryn Rexrode, one of the leaders of the study said,

'Our research suggests that women can reduce their risk of thrombotic stroke by up to 48% by eating fish two to four times per week.'

Further support for fish in the diet comes from the study reported in January 2001 in the *Journal of the American Medical Association*. The study concluded that women who consume as little as 225 grams of fish per week *cut their risk of suffering a stroke by as much as half.*

the balanced diet – juggling your carbs, protein and fat

In every women's and men's magazine, especially in every health, fitness and body-building magazine, you will see constant reference to the big three:

- **carbohydrates**
- **proteins**
- **fat**

They are constantly mentioned in terms of the balance between them, and are considered as vital as vitamins for your survival.

Why is this?

Carbs

Function: In addition to the health magazines, where do you most hear about 'carbs'? Amazingly, in computer and artificial intelligence magazines! It is vital in the context of silicon (the computer world) versus carbon-based (us!) intelligence.

We human beings are primarily made of carbon and hydrogen. It is therefore essential that our diets contain an adequate supply of carbohydrates – those foods which contain both carbon and hydrogen.

Found In: Primarily in *cell*ulose which are materials found in the *cell* walls of plants.

Holmesian Clue: **to keep your own body cells healthy, you need a diet that is rich in the cells of vegetables, seeds, nuts and fruits. They are not to be found in any animal products, nor in milk and milk products.**

Protein – the Ultimate Body-builder

Function: Protein is your personal, internal 'Body-Builder'. It is an organic compound, based on nitrogen, that has magical abilities to transform and adapt. This is why your body uses it as the main builder of your muscles, bones, organs and tissues. Without it you would be, literally, powerless.

Protein, like carbohydrates and sugars, is a major source of your energy.

It is important to know that protein is broken down by your body and distributed around it far more slowly than most other foods. So, when you eat protein you will not feel the sudden bursts of energy often associated with the intake of sugars, fats and some carbohydrates. The 'protein energy' builds up slowly, like a rising tide, and eventually reaches a level *at least as high as that of the sugars.* Unlike the sugars, and therefore to your tremendous advantage, the energy levels supplied by protein remain high for a long time. This means that if you add a bit more protein to your diet and decrease your sugar intake, you get a much more steady and powerful flow of energy throughout both your exercise period and your day.

Where do you find this super power food?

Found In: All whole grains, including peas, beans, seeds, nuts, rice; all pulses; root vegetables, including carrots and potatoes; most other vegetables (at lower levels); eggs; fish and meat

Summary of the 'big three'

You now know that a healthy diet must include the energy-boosting, power-providing, body-building 'Big Three' – fat, carbohydrate and protein. But in what proportions?

Happily, on this one everyone is in agreement – doctors, the nutritionists, beauty advisors, athletic coaches and body-building magazines included.

And what do they agree?

That carbohydrate is 'no. 1', protein 'no. 2' and fat 'no. 3'.

The proportions will vary, depending on the body type you desire and the amount and type of activity you wish to engage in. Happily, regardless of this, the range of variations in the proportions is quite small. Here are the recommended ratio ranges for a healthy, energy and power-producing Balanced Diet.

at last — the ideal diet solution

After decades — even centuries — of confusion and disagreement, the picture of a healthy human diet is becoming finally clear.

1 Vitamins
2 Calories
3 Fat
4 Ancestral habits
5 Human design
6 What the studies say
7 The balanced diet

Whether we look at it from the point of view of the eating history of humankind, our alimentary systems' design (the entire digestive tract), the essential vitamins we must have for survival, and the necessary Big Three — the nutritional requirements of all athletes, of fats, proteins and carbohydrate — *all investigations lead us to the same conclusions.*

Proportions and Content

Now that you have a very clear picture of what you are designed to eat, what you need to eat, and what type of foods to eat, what about the proportions? How much protein in relation to how much fat and carbohydrate? What proportion of vegetables to fruits, cereals, fish and meat?

Here again, the answers are happily straightforward.

Fat/Protein/Carbohydrate Ratios

Although the ratio may vary slightly according to your level of activity, this is the ratio to aim for to maintain a comfortable level of health.

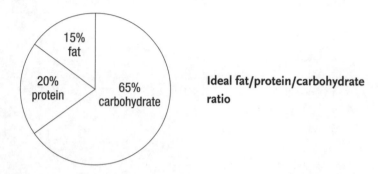

Ideal fat/protein/carbohydrate ratio

You now know that you *do* need fat as part of your diet. However, in view of the incredible efficiency of your body to translate fat into energy, you do not need that much. The guidelines are as follows:

Fat

If you are maintaining a comfortable level of health, but not pushing any boundaries, good fat should constitute a maximum of 15% of your diet. If you are extremely active and using between 3,000 to 5,000 calories per day, you can push this up to a maximum of 20% or, very occasionally, 25%.

Protein

As with fat, protein provides you with energy, and helps build your body, especially your muscles. Once again, in view of the fact that as an adult you have completed your major growth stages, and taking into account that your body is such an efficient energy converter, you do not need too much protein.

If you are at maintenance level good health, your diet should contain between 15% and 20% protein. If you are at full 'stretch', this percentage can go up to between 25% and a maximum of 30%.

Carbs

What is left? Carbohydrates! 'Carbs', as athletes often call them, need to form the basis of your healthy diet. This percentage should healthily range between 50% to 70%, and will supply you with the bulk of your vitamin and energy needs.

So now you understand about fats, proteins and carbs, how do you put this information into practice? What should you actually eat?!

Your Food Pyramid

Again, happily, there is a growing consensus on how your food pyramid should be constructed. In the latter half of the 20th century, the base of most recommended food pyramids was grains. As you now know from our 'eating history' the mass consumption of grains is a very recent development. Grains were never the staple of a hunter/gatherer's diet. This partly explains why hundreds of millions of people are allergic to wheat products. Many food pyramids (which tend to be devised by wheat and dairy producers!) still place them at the foundation.

The base of your food pyramid should be vegetables. Above that fruits, nuts and seeds, above that fish and meat, above that milk and grains, and at the peak, fats, oils and sweets.

Within this great pyramidal smorgasbord there are an infinite number of permutations and combinations of healthy meals you can eat! From now on, the experiment is yours to play with! Combine your diet with your exercise routines, look at and listen to yourself, explore new dietary combinations and forms with magazines, friends, and experts in the field.

And in the constant debate about whether you should eat to live or live to eat, which side do you think you should take?
Answer: both!

Drugs

What should be your approach towards drugs?

As with diet and all other matters concerning Physical Intelligence, you should adopt the approach of the two Os: Objectivity and Observation.

Using this formula will help you avoid much of the emotional confusion as well as the fear and hysteria that surrounds the subject of what to eat.

Simply defined, a drug is a substance which has a marked physiological effect when taken into the body. And clearly, drugs can be mild or strong, pleasant or unpleasant, and helpful or harmful in their effects.

As with our investigation into the ideal diet, examine the following evidence, so that you can intelligently come to your own conclusions. To make your job even easier, imagine that you are a Martian scientist, who has suddenly discovered the Human race. You decide to do an experiment in which you give them a series of substances, and observe the changes in their physiology, behaviour and life expectancy.

Water

Absence: death within a few days.

Moderate consumption: normal behaviour, normal life expectancy. All systems function normally and without defect.

Excessive consumption: excessive visits to the toilet! (Ultimately drowning!)

Food

Absence: death within a few weeks.

Moderate consumption: normal behaviour, normal life expectancy. All systems function normally and without defect.

Excessive consumption (especially of refined sugars, refined grains, dairy products and fats)**:** extreme obesity; risk of sudden death from heart failure; increased risk of heart ailments/attacks; cancers; diabetes; arthritis; general systems failure. Life expectancy reduced by 10–30 years.

Coffee/Caffeine

Absence: all systems function normally.

Moderate consumption: slight increase in hypertension, and slight depletion of essential nutrients.

Excessive consumption: hypertension; significant depletion of essential nutrients; increased risk of coupling excessive consumption with smoking. This is because of a false 'stimulation/relaxation' cycle. With excessive consumption of caffeine, the body intuitively knows that it needs to relax. When inhaling cigarette smoke, the body, which is expecting a fresh supply of oxygen with each inhalation, experiences a mini-asphyxiation, which momentarily numbs (mistakenly seen as 'relaxes') the body. Realizing that it is now in the process of dying, the body needs stimulation, and thus the next gulp of coffee. And so this dangerously negative spiral continues. Watch any of your friends who are addicted in this way, and you'll see that this habit is virtually robotic. Life expectancy is probably reduced by 2–5 years.

Cigarettes (Nicotine)

FACT: **By far the two most deadly risks to life in America are heart disease and cancer. The medical profession increasingly suggests that these are primarily caused by obesity, smoking and lack of physical activity.**

As a Martian, you observe that nicotine covers your lungs much like an oil slick covers the ocean, preventing the oxygen-breathing animals and organisms below it from surviving. Because of this assault on the system, general functioning and life expectancy are affected in the following ways:

1–20 cigarettes per day – A general increase in upper respiratory and cardiovascular ailments, with life expectancy reduced by 2 years.

20–40 cigarettes per day – A two-to-three-fold increase in the probability of most major ailments especially cancer, and a life expectancy reduced by 5–10 years.

40 cigarettes plus per day – A 5–10 times greater probability of most major ailments including all cancers especially lung; arthritis; asthma; colds; influenzas; all upper-respiratory ailments; lack of aerobic fitness; dramatic reduction in sense of taste and smell, and therefore reduction in refinement of memory; addiction, causing obsessive and irrational behaviour; inability to act with physical speed and stamina in cases of emergency; depression; halitosis! Rated by the United Nations as the world's second-most damaging drug to the individual and society at large. Life expectancy reduced by 12–15 years.

Other People's Smoke And Your Health

A Greek study published in the British Medical Association's quarterly specialist journal *Tobacco Control* confirms that being exposed to other people's cigarette smoke dramatically increases the risk of your suffering from heart disease.

The study found that people who never smoked had a 47% higher chance of developing acute heart disease if they were regularly exposed to the smoke puffed out by others. The risk grew exponentially with the number of years that non-smokers were exposed to other people's cigarette smoke.

Quitting – The Good News

A study published by Glaxo Wellcome confirms the resilience of your body to 'get back to normal' after quitting smoking. The encouraging news is that after:

20 minutes	Blood pressure and heart rate improve. Circulation improves in hands and feet making them warmer.
8 hours	Nicotine and carbon monoxide levels in the blood reduced by at least half. Oxygen levels return to normal.
24 hours	There is no nicotine left in the body! The ability to taste and smell is already improving.
48 hours	Carbon monoxide will be eliminated from the body. The lungs start to clear out mucus and other smoking debris.

	The chances of a heart attack begin to fall. Ability to taste and smell now greatly improved.
72 hours	Breathing becomes easier, more deep and more full. Airway passages in the lungs begin to relax. Energy levels increase.
2–12 weeks	Circulation improves, making walking and running easier.
3–9 months	Coughs, wheezing and breathing problems improve.
1 year	Risk of heart disease is reduced to about half that of a continuing smoker.
10 years	Risk of lung cancer falls to half of that of a continuing smoker. Risk of heart disease is similar to someone who has never smoked!
15 years	All systems functioning normally, and both risk of heart disease and stroke similar to that of someone who has never smoked.

The Glaxo Wellcome study also found that those who quit got a lot more out of life, including the following:

- Greater ability to cope with sudden exertion;
- Generally improved performance in all physical activities;
- Improved senses of taste and smell;
- Hair, clothes and skin smelling fresher;
- General appearance improved, with a healthy looking complexion

and no further smoke staining of fingers and teeth;
- A fresher less smoke stained house/car;
- A greater feeling of self-confidence – you have triumphed over addiction;
- Greater wealth! Smoking is an expensive habit – the average smoker (20 a day) spends about £100 per month on cigarettes. A heavy smoker £200 per month. That's between £1,000 and £3,000 per year!
- Quality of life improved with greater spending power.

Correctly linking behaviour with mind set, cigarette companies first attack your mind before attacking your body ... Dr Stanton Glantz of the San Francisco University Division of Cardiology says,

'The tobacco industry recruits new smokers by associating its product with fun, excitement, sex, wealth and power and as a means of expressing rebellion and independence.'

Despite the fact that the opposite is true, Sylvester Stallone signed an agreement with cigarette company Brown and Williamson worth $500,000 to use its products in five films. Twentieth Century Fox accepted $100,000 to promote Philip Morris products, giving the firm strict approval.

Use your Verbal Intelligence to protect your Physical Intelligence!

Marijuana

Absence: normal functioning.

Moderate consumption: feelings of 'highness'; increased tunnel-vision; decreased peripheral vision; decrease in short-term memory; tendency to social isolation; tendency to focused violence if provoked.
Excessive consumption: habituation; lethargy; increasing memory loss; chronic demotivation; cancer; panic attacks; damage to unborn babies; low sperm count; and other problems similar to excessive cigarette smoking. Life expectancy reduced 5–10 years.

Studies have shown that although most people are able to quit, 10–14% can become strongly addicted. Withdrawal systems are similar to those experienced by heavy smokers when they quit.

Ecstasy

Absence: normal functioning.
Moderate consumption: energy 'high'; increased heart rate and blood pressure; high thirst; post-experience exhaustion; increased probability of sudden death.
Excessive consumption: addiction; habituation cycle in which 'more produces less'; constant hypertension; accelerated systems function; overall systems burn-out; aggression; moral-less behaviour; greatly increased risk of sudden death. Life expectancy decreased by 5–20 years.

Cocaine

Absence: normal functioning.
Moderate consumption: similar to Ecstasy; significantly reduced sense of smell.

Excessive consumption: similar to Ecstasy. If 'snorted' can lead to complete burning out of the olfactory system and total loss of smell. Accompanied by panic attacks and addiction. Life expectancy diminished by 2–20 years.

Heroin

Absence: normal functioning.

Moderate consumption: almost immediate addiction. Hallucinations; random behaviour; loss of fine motor control.

Excessive consumption: major addiction; physical lethargy; anti-social behaviour; depression; loss of appetite; sudden death. Life expectancy reduced 5–30 years.

Alcohol

Absence: normal functioning.

Moderate consumption (2–3 glasses of wine per day, with meals, 4–5 days a week)**:** slight loss of sensory alertness; slight diminishing of verbal acuity; muscular relaxation; minor loss of inhibition; dilation of blood vessels. Life expectancy increased 1–2 years.

Excessive consumption: destruction of liver and skin (the body's biggest organ); sense of sight blurred, leading to temporary and sometimes permanent blindness; sense of touch numbed; sense of taste dulled; major diminishing of sense of smell; sense of hearing blurred; memory obliterated; sense of balance lost; physical co-ordination destroyed; speech function reduced by 60–100%; self-control absent (including urination, defecation and dribbling); social relationships permanently damaged or destroyed; highest probability of any drug of inciting domestic violence and abuse; increased risk of all major ailments; rated by the United Nations as easily the world's most destructive drug. Life expectancy reduced by 15–30 years.

The Monkey Is Not On Your Back – He's Inside Your Head!

Professor Michael Nader and colleagues at Wakeforest University in North Carolina has confirmed the popular belief that addiction to drugs is the preserve of those at the bottom of the social ladder rather than those at the top.

Professor Nader studied 20 male macaques (monkeys that are close relatives of human beings). The monkeys were initially housed in solitary confinement, and then in five groups of four. During their isolation, Nader looked at the animals' brains using PET scanners (positive emission tomography) and observed that the animals' brains showed very little difference in the way they processed dopamine. Dopamine is the neurotransmitter sometimes called the 'reward' or 'feel-good' chemical – a rush of dopamine provides a chemical 'high'. It is this physiological effect that drives addicts to feed their habit.

When the monkeys were housed in groups of four, social hierarchies quickly established themselves. Within only three months the quartets had acquired a firm pecking order. To Nader's surprise, the social clusters not only gave rise to different forms of behaviour (the dominant was the most aggressive; the bottom the most submissive), they also triggered a change in brain chemistry. In the dominant monkeys' brains, the number of dopamine receptors increased. 'The environmental consequences of those social hierarchies resulted in these changes,' said Nader.

When tempted with cocaine, a dopamine level-raising chemical, the dominant monkeys, whose leadership produced its own dopamine reward, took very little. The lower ranking monkeys, socially and dopamine deprived, consumed more.

One of the best ways to strengthen yourself in the battle against drugs, is to strengthen yourself!!

From this Martian perspective you will now be able to make far more objective and 'body-friendly' decisions about your own relationship with drugs. Strip them of their emotional entanglements, look at them with a clear inner eye, and, as with your diet, make decisions that are congruent with your own life goals and with the continuing development of your own Physical Intelligence.

Physical Intelligence Star – Paula Radcliffe

'You never know what may be possible until you take the risk and push forward. Only then can we find our own limits. We just don't know yet what our bodies will take and I'm not going to set limits for myself.'

Paula Radcliffe

If you had steadfastly run from the front in national, regional and world championships, as well as the Olympic games;

If you had done so for nearly 10 years and had always been overtaken in the final stages;

If you had never won a major championship of any sort;

If you had run your heart out in the last Olympics, leading all the way and thus acting as a pacesetter for the others, and, if, on the last lap, you were overtaken 1, 2, 3 ... leaving you in the ugliest and most depressing position of all, 4th;

If you had tried to rectify this in the world championships and had once again led all the way only, in the last lap, to be overtaken once again, 1, 2, 3 ... and ended, horribly, 4th again;

And if the world's press were labelling you 'cursed', 'the victim' and 'the loser' – would you give up?!

Yes, if you were the average person.

But not if you were the Physically Intelligent Star Paula Radcliffe.

Paula, with total dedication, took every defeat as an opportunity to learn and improve. She came back again and again and again, and, finally, the inevitable happened.

In one miraculous 12 month period she:

- Won, for the first time, the world cross-country championships. And then won it again!
- Won her second world half-marathon title.
- Entered, for the first time ever, a marathon – the London marathon. Everybody expected her to run from the front, hit the barrier, and as usual lose.

All the television commentators, including previous world record holders Brendan Foster and Steve Cram, were, by their comments, begging her to slow down as she strode out as usual, at the front. As sports writer Simon Barnes put it:

> 'And Paula ran and Paula ran, and the more she ran, the more it became clear that this was a dream from which there was no waking.'

Paula continued to run and run and, as millions of teary-eyed fans watched her, she crossed the finish line, recording by far the fastest time ever for a marathon debut and in a world record for the pure woman's marathon. As Barnes again put it:

> 'All of which put into perspective one of the greatest marathons ever run. Radcliffe's remarkable and utterly beautiful performance in the Flora London Marathon yesterday was given an added zing because of the pain of the past.'

- Four months later Paula ran in the 5,000 metres in the Commonwealth Games in Manchester and once again ran from the front. And one again Paula ran and ran and ran *away* from the opposition who had previously, in the last lap, pounced on her. Paula smashed the Commonwealth Games record and was only 3 seconds outside the world record.
- Nine days later, Paula entered the 10,000 metres in the European Games in Munich. Saying that she was carrying the enthusiastic roars of the Manchester crowd in her head, Paula once again led

the power of physical intelligence

from the start, once again ran and ran in the lead, and once again ran away from the lot! Her winning time of 30 minutes 1.09 seconds was the second fastest 10,000 metres of all time and obliterated the 16-year-old record of her heroine, the great Ingrid Kristiansen. As many reporters said at the time, the other greatest 10,000 metre runners in the world were beaten in body and mind by the unparalleled energy and determination of Paula. Neil Wilson of the *Daily Mail* described it as: 'The most destructive distance running ever seen from a woman in major competition.'

■ Two months later Paula once again did the impossible. Running in only her second marathon, Paula faced a very much in-shape Catherine Ndereba, the holder of the women's world marathon record of 2 hours, 18 minutes, 47 seconds. Paula led from the start, was 30 seconds inside the world record at the halfway mark, and then *accelerated*! Despite feeling nauseous in the 23rd mile, Paula maintained her astonishing pace (5 minutes, 16 seconds per mile) and smashed the world record by 1 minute, 29 seconds – the biggest world record improvement in 19 years. In the process, she thrashed every British male marathon runner! Everyone expected her to be shattered, but, on the contrary, Paula was ebullient, and within 10 minutes had hugged and congratulated everyone on her team, taken a mobile telephone call from her mother and conducted an interview for NBC!

How did such a 'loser' suddenly turn into a record-breaking world beater and the greatest women's long distance runner of all time?

The answer is that it wasn't 'suddenly'. For years Paula has monitored her body, and especially her diet. Treating her body much like Michael Schumacher treats his Ferraris, she has continually finely tuned her food intake, making sure that she consumes all the vitamins and nutrients she needs for optimal performance. In addition to this, she has tirelessly worked on her strength, flexibility, energy levels and stamina.

The result is a perfectly tuned and tough mind inside a perfectly tuned and tough body. Physical Intelligence and poetry in motion!

As well as Paula's determination, fighting spirit, focus, vision and unswerving belief in herself – 'I always believed I could win major events', she adds a sparkling personality and sense of humour to the mix. When asked to explain her latest round of victories, she quipped: 'I'm a late starter!'

For her supreme efforts, this 'late starter' was named Athlete of the Year for 2002.

DVD workout

This workout takes the form of key guideline tips to help you maximize your Physical Intelligence in this area.

Foods to Reduce

- **Wheat products.** Wheat contains gluten, a complex protein that many people find hard to digest. It can cause bloating and wind.
- **Dairy products.** Like wheat, dairy products are difficult to digest.

They can also cause bloating and flatulence. (*See* 'Ancestral Habits', page 93.)

- **Caffeine.** Caffeine is a stimulant which depletes the body of essential nutrients.
- **Refined sugars.** These give you an immediate energy burst and then leave you exhausted, having taken away more than they gave.
- **Excessive alcohol.** Increases free radical production and destroys Vitamins B, C and F. It also acts as a diuretic, prompting the kidneys to excrete more fluid and vital minerals.
- **Additional salt.** High salt intake can cause fluid retention, bloating and dehydration. It also increases the risk of high blood pressure.
- **Processed food with artificial additives.** Try to keep your diet as fresh and additive-free as possible.

Regular Detox

In the same way that your muscles need regular rest from exercise and activity, so your digestive system needs regular rest from foods that are tough to digest or 'unfriendly' to your body.

The recommendations for your diet in this chapter will go a long way towards giving you a 'detox' diet.

In addition, occasionally give your digestive system a complete break. Go on a 1–2 day water-only or grapefruit and water-only diet. This will give your body both the opportunity to rest, as well as to get rid of any toxins or any other rubbish it might have accumulated.

Experiment with your Diet

As well as giving your mind and body the variety it needs, certain exotic foods are especially healthy. For example, sea greens, often labelled 'super foods', contain more iodine than any other natural food. Iodine is needed by your thyroid to stimulate the nervous system and positively affect the rate of oxidation in your cells. This controls your metabolism and helps the body turn protein, fats and carbohydrates into energy.

Sea greens are also a good source of Vitamin B12, which is used to make red blood cells, which long-term vegetarians often lack, since meat is the usual dietary source of this nutrient. Sea greens (such as seaweed and other algae) also cleanse the intestinal tract, and because of the high mineral content work in the body to create more purified blood.

Become a Member of the Health-conscious World Community

Take heart from the fact that you are now a member of a rapidly growing community – the whole world is becoming more truly health/diet conscious.

A recent cover feature in *U.S.A. Today* reports that there is a massive rebellion against fast-food restaurants. Bruce Horovitz reports:

'The US$ 105 billion fast-food industry finds itself at a stomach churning crossroads that could affect the eating habits of almost every consumer in the nation – and ultimately the world. The fast-food titans are hearing, and responding to, a cry for more nutritious food.'

Says Ronald Shaich, CEO of Panira Red:

> 'They've all become self-service gasoline stations for the human body. If they aren't putting healthier things on their menus now, they'd be foolish.'

Further warns Eric Schlosser, author of *Fast Food Nation*:

> 'The time of the giants is past. The game will be won by regional chains that serve fresher, healthier foods.'

You are joining a band of growingly Physically Intelligent consumers!

Travel tips for Travellers

Make sure that when you travel long distances you are especially Physically Intelligent. Bad habits that many travellers fall into include:

- Frantically rushing, without taking any exercise, before traveling
- Gulping coffee before flying
- Exhaustedly lugging overloaded luggage
- Collapsing into the airplane seat with poor posture
- Over-indulging in alcohol on the flight
- Not drinking enough water
- Relentless immobile sitting on long flights
- Over-stuffing with fatty, sugar-laden and refined foods
- Neglecting exercise upon arrival

To avoid the resulting fatigue, dehydration, bloating, aches and pains, feelings of nausea, excessive 'jet lag' and even deep vein thrombosis, reverse all the above!:

- Exercise aerobically before you travel in order to aerate and invigorate and relax your body
- Make sure you are poised and balanced when carrying your luggage
- Drink plenty of water before, during and after flying
- Eat healthily on the plane, even taking your own healthy snacks/meal if necessary
- Drink alcohol sparingly
- Do in-seat flexing and stretching exercise, and regularly take walking/stretching breaks from your seat (minimum one per hour)
- Limit your caffeine intake
- Upon arrival, make sure you do at least half-an-hour of stretching/aerobic exercise to cleanse and rebalance your body's cardiovascular and muscular systems

Brain and Body Boosters

Browse through the following Brain and Body Boosters, selecting those that most appeal. Repeat one, two or three of these three times a day, especially as you are in the process of selecting your meal.

1 *I am increasingly aware of what constitutes a healthy diet.*
2 *What I eat is rich in the nutrients my body and mind need.*
3 *I am increasingly in control of my relationship with drugs.*
4 *I both eat to live and live to eat.*
5 *I am increasingly in control of my appetite.*
6 *The quality of the food I eat is the best I can obtain.*
7 *Fat is my friend; my relationship with it is a healthy one.*
8 *My Food Pyramid would make the Egyptians proud!*

chapter five

'A healthy body is a guest chamber for the soul; a sick body is a prison.'

Francis Bacon

Your magical body is made up of 10 super systems:

1	Muscular	6	Immune
2	Skeletal	7	Respiratory
3	Sensory/Nervous	8	Digestive
4	Endocrine (glandular)	9	Excretory (Urinary)
5	Cardiovascular	10	Reproductive

Each of your body systems is a group of connected parts, which includes organs and tissues; acting as a team, these carry out particular functions for you, such as breathing, movement and sensing.

These systems may be regarded as separate entities and processes within your body. However, each is completely dependent on the others for biochemical, functional and physical support. You can remain healthy and survive only if all your body systems are working together like a perfectly co-ordinated symphony orchestra – although your body is a billion times more complex than any known orchestra.

As you read 'All Systems Go' you will increasingly realize that you are a walking miracle!

Your Muscular System

When you are normally fit and healthy, your muscles make up approximately half of your body's bulk. Working with and supported by your amazing skeleton, your voluntary muscles (the ones over which you have conscious control) enable your body to make precise movements, to lift, to push, and to pull. They also enable you to use the most complex musical instrument ever devised – your voice – to communicate and to make the most beautiful music in song.

Your involuntary muscles, which work independently for you 24 hours a day to keep you alive, include your heart and smooth muscles. These provide the essential power for the functioning of your cardiovascular, respiratory and digestive systems. Already you begin to see the amazing interdependence of your body's major systems.

Each one of us is a wonderful metaphor for the possibility of global harmony!

It is also important to realize that coursing throughout your muscle tissue are millions of tiny capillaries which, through your blood, keep your muscles supplied with the abundant quantities of oxygen and glucose that are needed to fuel muscle contraction, and therefore for every move you make throughout your life. This emphasizes the importance of being aerobically fit.

Maintaining the strength, flexibility and power of your muscular system is vital. This is why *The Power of Physical Intelligence* has devoted the entire Chapter 3 to helping you to help your muscles help themselves!

Your Skeletal System

'God save me from the thoughts men think
In the mind alone;
He who sings a lasting song
Thinks in a marrowbone'

William Butler Yeats

Your skeleton provides you with your basic architecture – the framework within which and on which the rest of your body is built. The skeletal system is therefore essential to *all* your body's other systems.

Because we tend to see bones only after people have died, the common perception of them is as brittle sticks that are simply there to give us our shape. Nothing could be further from the truth!

Your bones are a living, 'breathing', incredibly strong *and* flexible system. In addition to providing you with structure, they are a fabulous nursery, where trillions of red and white blood cells grow, developing in a nutritious fatty (fat the friend!) tissue known as red marrow. When they are fully developed, they pass directly into your circulatory system.

Your bones also store, like a superb warehouse manager, essential minerals, including calcium. Your intelligent bones know exactly when to release them as and when your body has need of them.

In addition to being a tough, flexible structure that supports weight and vitally protects your internal organs, your bone tissue is constantly renewed, and, for an apparently 'rigid' structure, allows you an incredibly wide range of movement. Just think of the yogi, dancer, contortionist or gymnast! And your bones are *not* solid! They are composed of millions of tiny, interlinked caves that give them their amazing flexibility and strength.

So extraordinary are they, that Chris Williams, an architect at the University of Bath, is using their structure in the development of new arches, bridges and walls. He points out that nature has come up with bones and skeletons as a solution to most of the engineering problems that have faced architects throughout history, such as how to support loads and manage stresses. Williams says,

'There's no doubt the human skeleton is more efficient than any man-made structure.'

Just to give you some idea of the power you contain within you, the cartilage discs between the vertebrae in your spine can withstand enormous forces. This can be as much as *several hundred kilograms per square centimetre* during strenuous movements!

Your Brain/Sensory/Nervous System

When we are anxious we tend to call it a state of 'nerves' and, because of this, nerves have been given a bad press – as has the nervous system!

Your nervous system is about to be given a *good* press!

I am going to suggest to you that from now on you think of it as your '*brain/sensual-connection-with-the-universe*' system. For that is what it is.

Your body and brain are constantly alive with trillions of flashing electrical and chemical signals at the microscopic level. You are actually a walking beacon of light, emitting flashes of light, which, if compared with the night sky, would be blazing with trillions of meteors.

Your brain is literally the Crown of the system, and like a God-like puppeteer, it masterminds the rest of this astonishing system.

The system interacts intimately with every other of your body's major systems, and is the major highway for the billion-fold communication systems that go on between them every second of your life. Your nervous system therefore incorporates all the higher activities of your brain, including learning, memory, thinking and creativity, as well as providing you with every emotion and feeling of exhilaration you will ever experience.

In addition to this your nervous system includes:

- 200-million faceted eyes with which to see to the ends of the Universe;
- two ears with which to hear all song and music, including that of the spheres;
- an olfactory system that can pick out one molecule of aroma from billions;
- a tasting super-laboratory that can distinguish between millions of different taste sensations;
- a balancing mechanism that allows you to find unerringly your true centre of gravity;
- a super-sheath that allows you to see, through billions of tactile eyes, with your body's entire covering – your skin;
- an internal self-checking mechanism that monitors, second-by-second, every molecule of your being for health and maintenance;
- a 'night worker' billion-fold workforce which toils away for your benefit while you are asleep;
- an information storage system that can contain as much information as that in all the libraries of the Earth;
- a thinking super-biocomputer that is so fabulously complex that the combined genius of the human race to date is still only just beginning to understand it!

And that, dear reader, is just a *part* of you!

To function at maximum efficiency, the nervous system needs all the other major body systems to be working at full efficiency. Once again, healthy body–healthy mind; healthy mind–healthy body.

Your Endocrine (Glandular) System

The Endocrine System is an integrated network of hormone-producing glands and organs located in your head and torso.

Hormones are those complex chemical substances that are secreted into your bloodstream and regulate your body functions, including metabolism, growth and sexual reproduction.

Your Endocrine System is very much like a mini-body itself, with its own 'brain'.

Pituitary

The 'brain' of your endocrine system is the 'master gland' – the pituitary. Incredibly, the pituitary contains its vast range of masterminding skills in an area the size of a pea, and it has a phenomenal team of co-operative and supportive co-workers that toil in the super-factory of your body:

Hypothalamus

A major centre for memory, it produces hormones at the base of your brain which stimulate the other glands of the endocrine system to produce *their* hormones.

Pineal Gland

This tiny gland secretes *melatonin*, a mysterious hormone that influences sexual development and the health of your biggest organ – your skin.

Thyroid Glands

This gland controls your metabolism, including the maintenance of body weight, the rate of your energy use, as well as heart rate. This gland has the rare ability to store the hormones it produces.

Parathyroid Glands

You have four parathyroid glands at the back of your thyroid which produce the hormone that regulates your blood calcium levels.

Heart

Your heart produces a hormone called *atriopeptin*, which reduces blood pressure.

Adrenal Glands

You have one adrenal gland on each kidney. The adrenal glands produce several hormones that influence your body's metabolism and response to stress, including especially *adrenalin*, which gives you super-bursts of energy.

Kidneys

Your kidneys work in close association with your bones, especially the marrow. Hormones secreted by your kidneys stimulate the production of red blood cells in their cradle – your bones.

Pancreas

Your pancreas secretes hormones that control glucose levels in your blood, and therefore your energy levels.

Stomach

Your stomach is a major factory for the production of hormones which themselves stimulate the production of the enzymes that aid your digestion.

Intestines

Like your stomach, your intestines secrete hormones that play a major role in your continuing digestion.

Ovaries

The two ovaries in the female endocrine system produce the sex hormones *progesterone* and, most importantly, *oestrogen*.

Testes

The two testicles in the male endocrine system produce the male sex hormone *testosterone* which controls sperm production.

As you can see, your endocrine system is vital to your continued survival; it works in exceptionally close harmony with your cardiovascular system, and with your brain/sensual/nervous system. Your endocrine system also works in concert with and (effectively) as a part of your immune system (*see* Chapter 7).

Your Cardiovascular System

The cardiovascular system's basic function is to pump blood, and thus energy and life-giving oxygen, around your body. A pause of more than a few seconds in this life-supporting system results in loss of consciousness, and the rapid disintegration of the other systems.

It transports oxygenated blood to all of your body organs and tissues, and can adapt incredibly swiftly to changes in your environment and therefore in demand. This system also removes waste products from your body.

Your cardiovascular system is vital to your mental and physical stamina. I will cover it in far more detail in Chapter 8 – 'Physical Presence'.

Your Immune System

Your immune system helps to provide vital protection from the millions of invaders from the Universe. It also helps to maintain the proper function of all your internal tissues.

When you are robust and healthy, a beautifully intricate interrelationship of cellular, chemical and physical defences works as a barrier between you and continual external threats. Poor general health and weak companion body systems can compromise your immune system's efficiency. Healthy and vital companion body systems strengthen it against the invading hordes.

Chapter 7 – 'The I Team' is devoted solely to this vital system.

Your Respiratory System

Your respiratory system works in close harmony as the companion to your cardiovascular system. This system, like the circulatory, is a major part of your endurance and stamina, and is further developed in Chapter 8 – 'Physical Presence'.

Your Digestive System

Your digestive system is a masterpiece of engineering design. The digestive tract between your mouth and anus has a wide range of functions: the system checks out and takes in its chosen foods, breaks them down physically, and then digests them, breaking them down further into substances that are absorbed by your body cells. This system also eliminates every unnecessary substance that enters your body.

Health research is increasingly discovering that a healthy digestive system is dependent on a healthy and stable brain/sensual/nervous system. People often think of their digestive system as rather simple in comparison to the others. It is not! It is an amazing system, 30 feet long, starting with the mouth and continuing through the pharynx, oesophagus, stomach, small intestine, large intestine, rectum and anus. Associated digestive structures include three pairs of salivary glands, pancreas, liver, gall bladder, and circulatory system.

Throughout your digestive system, your veins and capillaries run like millions of tiny rivulets, exchanging information and energy on a second-by-second basis.

To illustrate the amazing physical and biochemical processes by which your digestive system breaks down your food and transforms it into myriad forms of energy would take diagrams so complicated that a map of their interactions would fill a wall the size of the side of a house – and it would still look like an impenetrable jungle!

Just one of the many miracles of your digestive system include your intestinal *villi* – millions of tiny projections that increase the surface area of your small intestine and which, if magnified, would look like a giant ocean floor covered with waving sea anemones and sea fronds.

As with all your other body's systems, the digestive system is essential to your survival. When it fails to co-operate with the other systems, illness and death result. When it is in fine health, it assists all your other bodily systems to maintain their excellent health.

Your Excretory (Urinary) System

The urinary tract is your body's filtering system. As blood passes through your kidneys, they create urine, which eliminates wastes and excess fluids from your body.

In addition, your urinary system also regulates the volume and composition of fluids in your entire body, keeping a delicate internal chemical balance.

In order to produce urine at the right rate, your kidneys are constantly alert and in communication with your cardiovascular system, your digestive system, your endocrine system, your various body rhythms and cycles, and your brain/sensory/nervous systems.

Your Reproductive System

The prime role of your reproductive system is to procreate – to produce offspring by generating and bringing together male and female sex cells.

In both the male and female, the reproductive process does not become fully functioning until your endocrine system, in conjunction with your brain, and the general state of health of your other bodily systems triggers rising levels of sex hormones which bring about physical sexual maturity.

As with all your other systems, your reproductive system is totally integrated with, and dependent on the healthy functioning of all your other bodily systems.

'all systems go' workout

The workout for all your body's delicate, sophisticated and astonishingly resilient systems is the accumulation of all workouts in *The Power of Physical Intelligence*.

If you train your mind to become strong, if you exercise your muscular system, if you eat a healthy and vitality-producing diet, if you avoid system-destructive drugs, if you walk with poise and elegance, if you maintain your mental and physical endurance and stamina, if you look after yourself as you age, and if you bring to bear your other Multiple Intelligences, all of your systems will be on 'GO!'

Physical Intelligence Star – Ian Thorpe: the Thorpedo

Not long ago Ian Thorpe was a 'dumpy little kid' who was so uncoordinated at ball games that he was everyone's last pick for their team. His father, who worked for a local council in Sydney sweeping leaves, reported that the boy was also allergic to chlorine!

Hardly the right ingredients for a boy who was to become the greatest swimmer of all time.

Within 10 years this kid had become:

- the youngest male swimmer ever to represent Australia
- the youngest male world champion at the World Championships
- broken four world records in four days at the age of 16
- broken 22 Olympic and World Records by the age of 19
- been voted 'the 'World's Most Outstanding Athlete'

How did he do it?

Answer: By having a clear personal vision of winning gold medals, by having a stated ambition in life 'to be the best I can be', by making sure that 'all his systems *can* go!' and by focussing on the balance between his body and mind and his sport and life.

Ian's dedication is absolute: His training consists of 10 sessions a week, 5 in the morning and 5 in the afternoon. His day starts with his alarm set to go off at 4.17 am in order to be in the pool by 5.00 am. In addition to these 10 sessions, Ian adds 2 weight-training (*see* Chapter 3) and 2 aerobic-based (*see* Chapter 8) stamina-enhancing boxing sessions.

As well as his rigorous training, the Thorpedo spends a lot of time working with his charity devoted to developing the body, mind and spirit of children around the world, as well as helping people find ways to fight cancer (*see* Chapter 7).

Described by his coaches as an avid learner, a flexible thinker, and a highly intelligent and well-rounded individual, the Thorpedo lives by the philosophy that you should be passionate about and love everything that you do.

So great is his energy that in the pool the men who trail him (which is nearly everyone!) say that it's like being immersed in a washing machine!

Ian's charity work and love for humanity extends to his prime life goal after swimming: to work for the United Nations. His reputation for honesty and moral certainty will stand him in good stead ... Sue Mott, sports columnist for the *Daily Telegraph*, said, 'Thorpe is the real thing, the embodiment of a gracious, charismatic champion. Wet he only is in the water.'

Brain boosters

1 *I am looking after and caring for my body's main systems in every way I can.*

2 *I am increasingly aware of the miraculous sophistication of my body's systems.*

3 *I am increasingly aware of the total integration of my body's systems with each other.*

4 *All my body's systems are increasingly healthy and strong.*

chapter six

'Everyone wants to be right, but no one stops to consider if their idea of right is right!'

Matthias Alexander

'The [next] great phase in man's development [is] when he passes from subconscious, to conscious control of his mind and body.'

Matthias Alexander

'A picture is worth a thousand words.'

Fredrick Barnard

---

walk tall

As you progress through *The Power of Physical Intelligence* you are beginning to realize that, once your mind has the right information, *you are the one in control*.

In this Chapter you are going to continue your role as a 'Body Detective' and will work through a number of self-examinations and self-checks to a formula that is used by all the Physical Intelligence Stars, especially the all-time greats in dance, sports and theatre.

Here is a short tale that will demonstrate to you that your brain is already 'set' to recognize what is excellent poise and performance, both for itself and for others.

'The Natural Eye'

While coaching junior, national, international and Olympic level rowers, I have the opportunity to attend many rowing regattas. At these I inevitably meet people who are 'there for the fun' but who 'know nothing' about the finer points of the sport.

They will often ask me which are the best teams and which teams I think will win. I always respond by asking them which teams *they* think look best, and which ones *they* think will win. Amazingly – but not so amazingly when you understand the nature of Physical Intelligence – they always pick exactly the same teams as an experienced rowing coach would pick.

Why is this?

Because the human eye is naturally tuned to pick out poise and balance. This is because it is necessary for survival to be able to do so.

And again, why?

Because any living being that is poised and balanced is going to be far more healthy, far more alert, and far more able to move. Such a being will be a much more valuable mate or friend, and a much more dangerous enemy!

You are now at the beginning of a fascinating study that will stay with you and help improve you for the rest of your life. I want you to use your natural awareness of poise to observe what it is about people (and other animals!) that demonstrates good poise. Be aware, look around you and consider what words you would use to describe people or animals that seem to you to demonstrate poise. Then think about words to describe those with poor poise.

self-check

Words that are often used to describe people and animals with poise, include:

Effortless	Elegant	Sublime
Graceful	Beautiful	Free
Balanced	Natural	Upright
Flowing	Inspirational	Light
Easy	Dance-like	Refined

On the other hand, words used to describe people or animals with poor poise include:

Slovenly	Slouched	Gangly
Uncoordinated	Sad	Depressed
Tired	Melancholy	Inefficient
Heavy	Ugly	Inelegant
Slothful	Static	Fixed

Which set of words would you rather have applied to you, your life and your family and friends?!

It is interesting to note that Leonardo da Vinci, arguably the most brain-balanced individual of all time, was also renowned for his extraordinary strength, exceptional poise, and the grace and balance of his movements. His physical grace was so extraordinary that people actually used to wait for him to walk from his house to his work, simply so that they could see and marvel at this paragon of excellence in bodily movement.

Poise as an Evolutionary High Point

Looking at the development of the hominids throughout the ages, you will notice something extremely interesting: that the more advanced the species, the more upright and erect its posture.

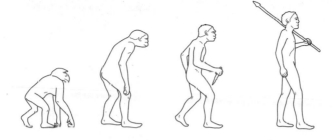

Why should poise give us such an advantage?

It all comes down to those words we use to describe a poised individual. Proper poise gives the body perfect balance, and thus allows you to move instantly in any direction. If your poise is poor and leaning forwards, sideways or backwards in any direction, you are immediately at a disadvantage when you need to make quick decisions and movements. Mohammed Ali was a perfect example of this, and he confounded everybody. Because he was so big they thought that such movement would be impossible. Totally untrue. Perfect poise allows for perfect movement, as Ali so artfully demonstrated. If the world had known more about Physical Intelligence and poise, they would have been surprised only that other athletes weren't all doing the same thing!

The Natural State

It is important here to emphasize that poise is the natural state. If you look at babies and very young children walking, running, carrying and jumping, you will notice that they walk and move in an upright position, beautifully, agilely and gracefully.

As the child progresses and is 'trained' to sit for long periods in uncomfortable or inappropriate seating, and as the fear of failure begins to spread like a disease throughout the body, posture gradually slumps, becomes misaligned, and the poses become more fixed and stylized. By the time they have become young adults they are often completely malformed!

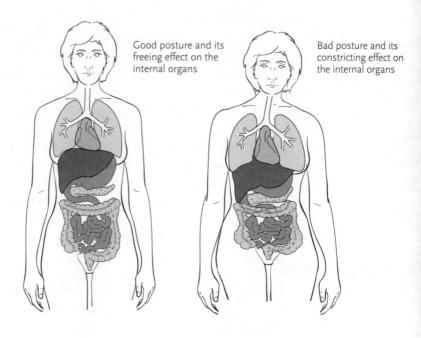

Good posture and its freeing effect on the internal organs

Bad posture and its constricting effect on the internal organs

the power of physical intelligence

This change in poise and bodily alignment takes place very gradually over the years, so it generally goes unnoticed.

If this process took place within 3 months, with the developing child becoming in that time unbalanced, distorted, muscularly and skeletally stressed, physically uncoordinated, less mobile and more rigid – and therefore all their sensory apparatus functioning far below par – imagine the international outcry and the *trillions* of pounds that would be dedicated to eradicating this scourge and curse!

The good news is that once your brain knows these facts, and has the correct information with which to make adjustments, it can realign itself towards its original and perfect poise.

Physical Intelligence Star – Tiger Woods

Once upon a time a two-year old little boy picked up a golf club and decided that he wanted to become the greatest golfer in the world! This was no idle dream. By the time he was five he already had a picture of his greatest hero, Jack Nicklaus, on his bedroom wall. His bedroom walls began to fill – with tables, charts, graphs and more photographs of every single accomplishment and record achieved by the greatest golfer the world had yet known.

The little boy grew up, compiled the best amateur record in history and turned professional in 1996.

Of all the Nicklaus records that Tiger Woods wanted to beat, the most formidable was Jack's 18 major victories between the ages of 22 and 46. Tiger already has 7 between the ages of 21 and 26!

His second major goal was to catch Sam Sneed's 81 US PGA Tour victories. In 6 years Tiger has 31 at which rate he will have reached Sam's 81 in another 10 years although he has probably 20 or 25 more playing years to catch him.

In his first 6 years Tiger:

- Had the lowest average scores in the PGA
- Established ranking points that were twice that of the number two player
- Won 31 PGA events and 7 Majors. For major wins he is already tied with golfing greats, Arnold Palmer, Sam Sneed, Gene Sarazen, Harry Vardon and Bobby Jones
- Won 30 out of 33 tournaments in which he was leading going into the final round.
- Also established himself as the longest and most powerful hitter in the game
- Won four Majors in a row, an accomplishment now called the 'Tiger Slam'
- Has been voted Golfer's Player of the Year 3 times!

In a short period of time, he also won 6 of the last 9 majors and 8 of his last 16 tournaments. The No.2 player in the world, Phil Mickelson, hasn't won one!

For his prodigious accomplishments Tiger has been *twice* proclaimed *Sports Illustrated* World Sportsman of the Year.

So outstanding and poised is he in competition and victory, that in 2002 a move to 'de-Tiger' courses was started at Augusta where the Masters was held.

Tiger thrashed the field for his seventh major victory demonstrating that he can win such events under any conditions, long course or short, wet or dry, wind or dead calm.

As the *International Herald Tribune* commented:

'In all of sports, the expression "he's so good it's scary" may only truly apply to Tiger Woods. Doesn't he ever crack or make a poor decision when it counts? Doesn't he ever reach the bottom of this well of will? If he's a fully functioning human, utilizing every iota of his potential, where does that leave the rest of us?

'Tiger's impeccable victory in Augusta, after husbanding his emotional fuel since last year's Slam, only underlines the degree to which his every deed and decision is part of a project which began when he was two and still extends to the horizon.'

When asked what advantages he thought Tiger Woods had over other players, Jack Nicklaus commented that he only had *one* advantage,

'He's a better player than everybody else! That's a pretty good advantage.'

Nicklaus and others also commented that the biggest obstacle to golfing achievement is life management, and that Tiger is on his way to becoming a master of that also.

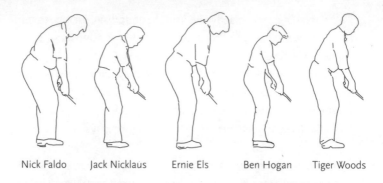

Nick Faldo   Jack Nicklaus   Ernie Els   Ben Hogan   Tiger Woods

Even among the greats of golf, Tiger's poise is outstanding and is the prime reason why he is being hailed as the greatest golfer of all time.

So how does Tiger excel with such elegance, grace and poise? As you might have guessed, Tiger has a Method to his Magic.

I will now take you step-by-step through Tiger's own 'How to Win' formula. Compare it with what you have learned so far in *The Power of Physical Intelligence* and with your own growing Holanthropic conclusions!

1 **Mental toughness and control** – Tiger started training his mind right from the start. As he says, 'Control yourself and you control your destiny'. He is an avid learner and has said of his mind that it is a 'computer with thousands of megabytes of memory.'

2 **Strength** – When he first turned professional, he was light for his height. 'One minute I would hit a nine iron 150 yards and the

next 170'. Tiger developed his muscles in order to achieve consistency. He reports, 'I developed a physical fitness routine that would allow me to work every part of my body. I wanted to have effortless power and the ability to hit little finesse scoring shots. My intention was to work every muscle so I would not only increase my strength, but my endurance too'.

3   **Diet** – Again, as you might imagine, Tiger eats a well-balanced diet of the sort you investigated in Chapter 4. Other habits he has trained in himself – drinking plenty of water, avoiding too much sugar and salt, avoiding heavy foods when he is training, and avoiding late meals. Tiger also avoids drugs.

4   **Flexibility in Body and Mind** – Tiger emphasizes physical flexibility and, as Mark Reason, golf correspondent said, 'Woods has a healthy obsession with his body'. Tiger particularly admires and follows the example of Sam Sneed, who was one of the most flexible athletes ever. Sam could kick the top of an 8-foot ceiling when he was 75-years old and could touch his left thumb against his left forearm without help from the other hand. (You try it!) Tiger intends to emulate him.

5   **Endurance and Stamina** – Tiger regularly runs 3–5 miles, and if he is not able to, he uses a stationary bicycle. He reports, 'When I first started on the bike, I had to set it almost at beginner's level. Now I can ride that baby at nearly the maximum level of difficulty'. Tiger said that he learned the value of staying in shape as a youth when he was running cross-country, and has applied those lessons to his golfing supremacy. As well as physical

presence, Tiger also focuses on mental persistence, having been trained by his Dad and himself to nurture a 'relentless, never-ever-give-up attitude'.

6 **Positive Thinking/Failure** – Tiger is a relentlessly positive thinker, and believes that you have to have a total belief in yourself as well as an ability to live with the outcome of your efforts, whether they are good or bad. He says, 'The road to failure is paved with negativity. If you think you can't do something, the chances are you won't be able to. Conversely, the power of positive thinking can turn an adverse situation into a prime opportunity for heroism'.

Tiger demonstrated that he practises what he preaches when, after a disastrous worst round of his life – 81 at Muirfield in the Open – he immediately bounced back with the best round of the day, 65, and following that he won his next tournament!

Tiger's dedication to his mental and physical fitness has put other top golfers in a mental no-where land. Thinking in exactly the opposite way that *The Power of Physical Intelligence* recommends, Colin Montgomery, one of the world's top 10, recently said: 'You're not going to beat Tiger mentally; you are not going to beat him physically. You are not going to beat him by outdriving him. You are not going to beat him by putting, chipping or iron play.' Other defeatist talk came from the world No. 3 Ernie Els who said: 'When I have played well, Tiger has still beaten me. What do you do? I think this guy is just a totally

different talent than the world has ever seen. I work hard at
everything in my game. And when I've had it going, I got beat.
Maybe I'm not good enough.'
Tiger, like the Williams sisters, has won before he even gets to the
first tee!

Els also mentioned the transformation of the health of the
professional golf players in which Tiger has led the way, 'You
don't see guys with fat bellies out there any more. Guys are fit
and strong'.

7   **Humour and Fun** – as well as being focused, like other great
Physically Intelligent individuals, Tiger has a great sense of fun,
and never finds his work and play boring.

In one tournament in Germany, where other players were hopeful
that Tiger would arrive jet lagged enough to let someone else win,
Tiger told them not to count on it. With a smile he said, 'I *love* to
travel!'

Tiger also says that the game (of golf or life) should never be boring,
especially when you're working to improve. He said, 'I have just as
much fun on the practice range and green as on the golf course. I love
working on shots, carving them this way and that, and proving to
myself that I can hit a certain shot on command.'

With his complete focus on his mental powers and physical
excellence, Tiger is the living embodiment of Ralph Waldo Emerson's
statement:

'He who throws himself unhesitatingly on his thought, instantly rights himself, stands in the erect position, commands his limbs, works miracles.'

Neuroscientists at the California Institute of Technology in Pasadena have discovered that it is not only your eye that gives you your sense of direction – it is your eye in combination with information your brain receives from neck and head movement. In an experiment, people were divided into two groups. The first group was allowed to see things moving in front of them, while their head and neck were held rigid. The second were shown exactly the same scenes, but were allowed to move their head and neck appropriately.

The second group performed far better.

This research confirms the vital importance of the relationship between the head, neck and back. If these are held rigid, as is the case with many people who have poor poise, not only do muscular skeletal problems arise; perception is both diminished and less accurate.

poise workout

Now that you are more fully aware of the great importance and impact of poise for your personal physical fitness and health, how do you maintain and improve yours? Find out the answers in the following Poise Workout.

Remember Shakespeare's phrase: 'All the World's a Stage ...' From now on, when you are people-watching, notice whatever it is you normally notice *plus* their poise, balance and physical alignment. You will be surprised at just how many of us have literally been bowed down by the weight of inappropriate Physical Intelligence habits and failure.

You will also be amazed at how many beautifully poised people there are. Admire them! Study them! Copy them!

1 Look at photographs of poised people and animals and use them as your beacons. All great Physically Intelligent Stars, as you will already be becoming aware from reading their stories, had examples on to which they latched their own dreams.

2 You can do the same!

3 Regularly check your own body and the positions of your limbs and joints in relation to each other. One good way to do this is to work your way from the top to bottom or bottom to top of your body, checking the joints and major muscle groups, to see if there is any tension, stiffness or locking. If there is, don't worry. *Gently* allow your body to unfold and open into a more poised position.

4 Occasionally, when you are walking or engaging in athletic activity, imagine that your head is much lighter than it actually is, more like a helium-filled balloon. This will make your head feel more buoyant and will allow the rest of your body to bear the weight more easily.

To realize why, think of those people who carry massive loads of produce on their heads. If their heads were even one centimetre off pure poise, the weight would be unbearable. With pure poise, the weight is easy to carry. It is the same with your head itself!

5   Stand naked in front of a mirror and 'check yourself out'. With your imagination, superimpose a perfectly poised body in front of that mirror and check for your own alignment. When you have observed any differences between you and 'perfection' gently make adjustments, allowing your own mind and body to become comfortable in this new position. This way you will be creating and training the habit of good poise.

6   Investigate the martial art of Aikido, which is based on poise and balance. Its founder, Morehei Ueshiba, who devised aikido (the way of harmony) by studying human poise and movement, is famed as one of the most poised and balanced martial artists of all time. When he had perfected his study, he, as was his privilege and right as a National Treasure, called together the top people in Japan for a demonstration. In the demonstration he was attacked by four senior black-belts in the martial arts. With incredibly little movement or apparent effort, Ueshiba was easily able to subdue them all, in the process making sure that none of them was in any way hurt.

This new martial art, based on poise, balance, 'reading' your attacker's body signals and language, and on sensory alertness, flexibility and maximum and efficient use of strength, was so powerful that it was immediately incorporated into the training of the Royal Guard, and was kept secret from all others.

It has now become one of the fastest-growing physical and health-training movements in the world.

Its principles are completely in tune with the principles of

Physical Intelligence. Aikido will give you a complete Holanthropic (body and mind) workout ...

7 Flexibility. If you are poised you will naturally be more flexible, because all your joints will be more open, your muscles more relaxed, and your entire body more free to move in any direction you choose. You can 'top up' this flexibility with the study of such disciplines as aikido, yoga, gymnastics and dance. Whenever you are studying these, always bear in mind the basic principle of Matthias Alexander, the master of poise, who stated that you must always: 'allow your neck to be free so that your head may go forward and up, and your back may lengthen and widen.'

In other words, stay poised and balanced in whatever flexibility and other exercises you do.

Brain boosters

1 *I move with increasing poise and grace.*
2 *I regularly look out for, observe and study examples of good poise. I emulate them.*
3 *Gravity is my friend.*
4 *The excellence of my poise positively affects the excellence of my overall physical and mental performance.*
5 *I am allowing my neck to be free so that my head may go forward and up and my back may lengthen and widen.*
6 *I walk tall!*

---

chapter seven

'… doctors believe that as much as 70% of all chronic diseases in the United States of America – from diabetes and high blood pressure to heart disease and even some cancers – can be warded off with some timely, sensible changes in lifestyle.'

Christine Gorman

'Early to bed early to rise makes one healthy, wealthy and wise.'

proverb

'Health is the condition of wisdom, and the sign is cheerfulness, an open and noble temper.'

Ralph Waldo Emerson

'The natural role of twentieth-century man is anxiety.'

Norman Mailer

'How much have cost us the evils that never happened!'

Thomas Jefferson

'Worry gives small things a big shadow.'

Swedish proverb

In the same way that astronomers are discovering great new systems and beautiful structures in the Universe, so biological science is discovering wondrous new systems in your human body.

One such miraculous system is your immune system. To get a good picture of how huge and powerful the armies of your immune system are, imagine every soldier in every war ever fought, combined with every military force in every science-fiction empire ever written about or filmed, and combine them all into one great intergalactic army. This army, in both number and originality of weaponry, would pale into insignificance beside the trillions of warriors who daily fight on your behalf!

You are their leader, and they need your brilliant leadership, constant vigilance and love if they are to defend you to the maximum of their capability.

The major feature of your immune system is your lymphatic system.

This system's 'blood', the lymphatic fluid, circulates the trillion-fold defence force around your body. The lymphatic arteries, veins and capillaries roughly parallel the path of your blood's circulation systems. In the organs, they follow the arteries and often, like tender vines, form networks around them.

Also mirroring your endocrine system, your immune system has many special organs which serve as 'command centres' to fend off invaders. These include:

Tonsils

These glands and the adenoids produce antibodies against ingested or inhaled organisms.

Lachrymal glands

These glands produce tears that contain an enzyme that helps protects your eyes.

Salivary glands

These produce saliva which is one of the most lethal 'swamps' into which any unfriendly organism can wander. The tar pits that trapped the dinosaurs were mild by comparison!

Spleen

The largest of your immune organs the spleen produces trillions of antibody soldiers as well as filtering out damaged red blood cells.

Stomach

An acid and enzyme bath from which very few unfriendly invaders escape!

Bone marrow

In the same way that bone marrow is the cradle of red blood cells, the standard immune system blood cells – the lymphocytes, commonly known as the normal white blood cells, begin their life as stem cells in your bone marrow. The giant nanocytes, the largest of the white blood cells, are also born here. The multiple trillions of white blood cells, some of your most ferocious fighters, migrate into tissue spaces where they develop into scavenger cells that comfortably defeat and devour the toughest bacterial invaders. They also feast on any other dead cells that could jeopardize your health.

And it doesn't stop there! Your immune system has an incredible arsenal of further weapons to fight off invaders. It:

- 'freezes' them to death
- 'boils' them to oblivion
- devours them
- strangles them
- suffocates them
- drowns them
- poisons them
- ejects them
- cripples and maims them
- eviscerates them

- explodes them
- disintegrates them
- dissolves them
- imprisons them
- starves them
- inactivates them

In addition to these phenomenal forces, the immune system also has 'sleepers'; these are like super biological landmines that can lie in wait for years until the right response-triggering enemy dares to invade. The 'sleepers', like monsters from the deep, suddenly burst into life and eliminate the invaders.

As you have learnt, your armies need supply lines. You are the Emperor or Empress who provides and sustains those. Your immune system warriors need you to feed them well. They need your bones to be healthy and strong in order to supply them with more fresh and powerful warriors. They need your muscles to be flexible and powerful in order to circulate them to all the parts of your body that need defending. They need a healthy supply of oxygen and red blood cells to give them energy in their ceaseless battles on your behalf. They need a digestive system that is efficiently processing all the nutrients that give them added energy in their campaigns. And they need a brain, and a sensory and nervous system that is alert, open, relaxed and free from stress.

Give them that chance; that gift.

Aerobic Training, Sleep and Stress

In addition to improved volume and higher quality of blood, aerobic exercise also increases the blood supply to each of your billions of muscle cells.

With a greater volume being pumped through with a greater power in every beat, the body once again realizes that its old, unfit cardiovascular system can no longer take the strain. In response, all your blood vessels become larger and more flexible, thus making the passage of blood through your body much easier.

Another miraculous thing now occurs. Your new and stronger-pumping heart puts pressure on the tiny veins and capillaries at the very edges of your cardiovascular system near the surface of your skin. In the same way that a swollen river forges new rivulets, so your body responds by creating millions of new capillaries near the surface of your skin (your body's largest organ). These new capillaries supply the vital boundary between you and the Universe with fresh vigour to breathe, respond to all forms of stimuli, and fight off hordes of microcosmic invaders.

Aerobic exercise will also increase the quality of your sleep and will often lessen the amount you require.

Exercise and Sleep

In a seminal study, Dr Cooper had two groups of people stay in bed, flat on their backs, for three full weeks. The first group exercised three times daily on bicycle ergometers that were strapped to their beds; the other group was allowed no exercise.

The results were that the exercise group had normal sleep patterns throughout, sleeping 7–8 hours a night. The group which was not allowed to exercise slept erratically, or occasionally developed chronic insomnia. In a finding that appeared to go against common sense – but which is predictable if you know about the nature of your body and brain – the group that had not exercised actually wanted to sleep for *longer*. When they were awake, even after having had more sleep than the other group, they were still comparatively listless. The aerobically-trained group slept less *and* were more alert during the day.

When you are aerobically fit, you give your brain a deeper and more meaningful rest and integration period, for one quarter to one third of every day; the remaining 67–75% of the day is then spent in a state of higher sensory and intellectual alertness and awareness.

This combination of good aerobic exercise and excellent rest is an ultimate feast for your immune system, and will greatly strengthen it, reducing the risk of ill health.

The negative effects of stress are very similar to those of bad poise. Your body gets 'pulled down'; your blood vessels constrict; your muscles tighten; your nervous system overreacts; your glands pump out too little or too much of their precious stores; breathing becomes short and inefficient; your senses become diminished; sexual appetite declines; mood deteriorates; and your brain becomes relatively addled!

Physical Intelligence Star – Lance Armstrong

Imagine that as a young man at the age of 26, you are told that you have cancer. Not a mild cancer, but one that started in your testicles, spread to your abdomen, then to your lungs, and finally to your brain.

Imagine then that you were told you had less than a 20% chance of surviving (and this is an optimistic estimation!), that you had to undergo months of chemotherapy and radiotherapy, and, in addition, that you had to have your brain operated on to extract the vicious tumour.

Imagine then that you are asked if you would mind competing, in less than 2 years' time, in 20 marathon races spread over 24 days. Not only that, but you are expected to win the overall total of all those marathons.

And not only *that* – you are expected to do this for 4 consecutive years in a row.

Someone did have all those cancers and someone did ask that someone to compete in those marathons. The person who had the cancers was Lance Armstrong; the person who asked him to compete and win was himself!

And he did!

Lance Armstrong has won 4 consecutive Tour de France bike races in which the riders race for 20 days over distances that often exceed 200 km. Some days the races are on the flat. Some days the races are up the steepest mountains in the Alps and Pyrenees. Sometimes the races are against the clock. In each type of terrain, there is usually a group of specialists.

Lance Armstrong has won them all!

How did he do it?

By mind over matter, by incredible acts of will, by a phenomenal all-round physical training programme and by his acquiring a complete knowledge of his body and its dietary and psychological needs. In so doing he built up one of the most phenomenal immune systems the world has ever known.

In trying to answer why Armstrong was so dominant, the *Herald Tribune* noted:

> 'A combination of speed and power may be enough to win the Tour de France, as many riders have proven, once. To prove it 4 times, a rider needs to add focus, consistency, dedication … and health. Of these, dedication might be the foremost. Asked recently when he would begin preparing for the next season (after having just won the Tour de France), Armstrong replied, "I've already started."'

Like Tiger Woods, Lance's attitude towards failure or defeat is to learn from it and then to excel. Lance's Director Sportif, Johan Bruyneel, likes to tell the story of Lance's training rides on the Joux Plan, an Alpine climb where Armstrong faltered on his way to overall victory in 2000, the only bad day he has had in the last 4 Tours de France. Although the Joux Plan was not on the itinerary for 2002, Armstrong was training there in the spring, working on conquering his conqueror. He rode up it once, turned around at the peak, barrelled down and climbed it again. That day he spent 8 hours in the saddle, suffering terrible fatigue. A few days later, Armstrong won the Joux Plan stage in the Dauphine Libere Race!

It is no coincidence that Lance, like all the other Physical Intelligence stars, is never interested in resting on his laurels – he is always trying to strive for improvement. He uses Michael Schumacher's sport as a metaphor:

> 'We take a Formula One approach. Formula One teams are always testing, always
> tinkering. Testing the brakes, testing the tyres, testing the engine, always trying to
> improve. That's us, too.'

Lance's whole attitude can be summed up by the fact that when he was
first told of his serious cancers, he decided, despite the tiny probability of
his living, to label himself, not a cancer victim, but rather a 'cancer
survivor'.

Using the awesome power of his Physical Intelligence he has held
that monster at bay for 6 years and accomplished physical feats which,
in the context of his health history, are miraculous.

Mental Attitude

Your mental attitude has a direct correlation with both your physical
health, your mental fitness, and the strength and vigour of your
immune system. An attitude of fear, indecision, indifference,
inflexibility and negativity produces stress, ill health and a generally
deteriorating set of mental skills. Studies by the British Medical
Association and American Medical Association have shown that as
much as 80% of disease is caused by negative mental attitudes that
weaken the armies of your immune system.

FACT: **In America, 'blind' teenage girls see fat where there is none!
This is reflected in the percentage of girls who say they think
they are overweight, compared with the percentage who
actually are.**

Age	Think they are overweight	Actually overweight
14	33.4%	7.7%
15	35.6%	6.6%
16	35.2%	6.7%
17	35.9%	6.3%

An open-minded, committed, flexible, curious and optimistic mental attitude will produce a body that is physically more healthy and free from stress, a robust immune system and a mind which is more alert and capable of dealing with the constant 'intelligence tests' with which the planet Earth challenges your brain every hour of every day.

Brain boosters

1   *My immune system is the size of a galactic army!*
2   *As I improve my relationship with stress, I am strengthening my immune system.*
3   *I am supplying the warriors of my immune system with the nutrients they need to keep them healthy and strong.*

chapter eight

'Scientists have found that when hitherto sedentary 40-year-old women who start walking briskly (aerobically!) for half-an-hour a day, four days a week, they enjoy almost the same low risk of heart attack as women who have exercised conscientiously for their entire lives.'

Time Magazine, 5 February, 2001

'We know that if everybody exercised a few hours a week, type two diabetes would be virtually non-existent.'

Dr Ken Goodrick, Associate Professor, Baylor College of Medicine, Houston

Two of your body's 10 major systems are vital for your endurance and stamina: your cardiovascular system and your respiratory system, both of which are intimately linked in supplying your body with the necessary stamina-fuel: oxygen. Your cardiovascular system's basic function is to pump a supply of oxygen, via the red blood cells in your blood, to all those parts of your body that need it, especially during vigorous activity and exercise.

Your respiratory system, working in immaculate conjunction with your breathing muscles, is the means by which the cardiovascular system gets its necessary supply of fuel and energy. Like all your other body's systems, both of these are magical in their complexity and sophistication.

Fortunately, like your muscles, these two systems can be trained and strengthened to give you extraordinary endurance and stamina.

The rest of this chapter will tell you how. First, let's get rid of some false beliefs.

**False belief: 'Work up a good sweat for a competition or contest.'
Truth: Quite simply, sweating takes energy.** You want to conserve, not lose energy: especially before a contest, Therefore, do gentle warm-up exercises, and practise skill-warm-ups before an event. The two reasons why prolonged warm-ups and working up a good sweat are counterproductive are that they deplete your nutritional stores and they heat-sap the energy that you need in the competition.

Let the sweating take place during the event!

Dr Kenneth Cooper, a young and brilliant medical doctor, who was also a considerable athlete/runner himself, had graduated from the Harvard School of Public Health, and was working at the United States Air Force School of Aerospace Medicine in Texas.

I had the pleasure of meeting him some years later, and he told me the incredible story that defined his life's work, which shattered many of the illusions about what 'physical health and fitness' meant, and which changed forever the way we look at training and nurturing our bodies.

He told me that the United States Armed Forces had begun to report a very worrying phenomenon. Some of their strongest, fittest and apparently healthiest young soldiers, sailors and pilots were dying from causes that remained a mystery. A disturbing by-product of this finding was from the autopsies. When the internal organs of the fit young men were examined, they often appeared to be from a much older body – sometimes as much as 10 years older.

How was it possible that in an apparently fit and healthy young body, its actual medical condition was of a body considerably older? It didn't appear to make sense. You would expect the opposite to be true.

how aerobic training transforms the inner you

Forms of exercise that particularly help you become aerobically fit, and which, when you do them well, are extremely enjoyable and satisfying, include:

- swimming
- fast and long-distance walking
- running
- long-distance skiing
- dancing
- rowing
- making love

There is also a growing range of aerobic training machines that mimic a number of these activities.

Your 200 bones, 500 totally co-ordinated muscle systems incorporating billions of muscle cells, over 11 kilometres of nerve fibres, and your unbelievably sophisticated cardiovascular system are all eagerly waiting for you to give them the 'go' sign in order that they may best serve you!

The Effects of Aerobics on the Heart

If you train for only 10–15 minutes per session, your brain and body will say to themselves something like: 'Oh, this is a little bit difficult, but it's not going to last for long. No need to change.'

As you have learned, your body is designed to adapt and change. The most common example of this is with skin calluses. If you have done no manual labour for some time, and then suddenly go into an enthusiastic bout of gardening and digging, your hands will become callused. Why? Because your brain has received alarm-bell messages that this part of the body is now being used excessively, and the soft skin of the hands is not up to the task. The body and brain combine to toughen up the area taking the strain.

It is this phenomenal ability of your system to adjust itself to the stresses and strains being placed on it that is the basis of aerobic training and all muscular development. This is why the 20 minutes is so vital. When you maintain a high heartbeat for this duration of time, a sustained message is sent to your brain and body that they are in danger of running out of oxygen. This is life-threatening!

As a result, a 'red alert' message goes out to all systems instructing them to 'crank up' in order to deal with the increased demands.

The first effect of good aerobic training is that it increases the size and strength of your body's most important muscle – your heart. Studies have shown that an athlete's heart is larger, stronger and more healthy than average. It becomes highly efficient, and pumps more blood with each beat and with less effort. A heart that is unexercised is smaller, weak – like any unexercised muscle – and possesses smaller chambers into which the blood flows and from which it is pumped out.

In a happy synergetic design of nature, your heart, in addition to feeding the rest of your body, feeds itself. Your coronary arteries, which feed your heart muscle its own supply of blood and oxygen, are correspondingly stronger when your heart is healthier. It is a wonderfully positive feedback loop. Your stronger heart feeds itself a stronger supply of nutrients, which makes it even stronger, which allows it to become physically more powerful and to supply even better nutrients and so on in a positive spiral of health.

In addition, your fitter heart will beat more slowly, pumping out a greater volume of blood and oxygen with every beat. When your heart is healthy it will beat at 60 pulses per minute or less, whereas when your heart is unfit it will beat at 80 or more pulses per minute.

It really is like the ultimate athlete, who works more effortlessly, gracefully and efficiently, while the lesser athlete struggles behind, expending energy in all sorts of inefficient ways and with far more effort, producing far worse results. Like the ultimate athlete, your aerobically fit heart will not only be more efficient in times of extreme demand and exertion, but it will also be more efficient in periods of relaxation and normal activity. A further benefit is that, again like the superior athlete, your healthy heart will have exceptional stamina and endurance.

The Effects of Aerobic Training on Your Lungs

Your lungs are composed of many millions of tiny grape-like globes called alveoli. These are surrounded with a network of fine blood vessels – the capillaries. Oxygen-containing air is drawn into the alveoli. When you inhale, your capillaries, like little hungry creatures, devour the oxygen. When you exhale, the remaining air plus waste products from your blood, such as carbon dioxide, are eliminated.

The oxygen is carried around your body by the haemoglobin in your red blood cells. Not surprisingly, the ability of your lungs to function and to supply your body with the much needed oxygen, is entirely dependent upon the 'breathing fitness' of the muscles of your rib cage and diaphragm. These 'breathing muscles' can get fit *only* by aerobic training. They also obviously work better if you are physically poised.

Further evidence of the validity of the *mens sana in corpore sano* principle comes from a study by Dr Appleton and Dr Kobes at the United States Military Academy at West Point. They made a study that directly compared the physical aptitude and health of their cadets and their success at the academy. Over four years, the cadets who were fit had an attrition rate half that of their unfit classmates. The dropout rate was also especially high among non-athletes, who found themselves incapable of absorbing the academic curricula – simply because they did not have the alertness and stamina to maintain the necessary mental effort.

Similar tests have shown highly positive correlations between performances in physical tests and exercises, and academic and leadership qualities. They have also revealed a positive correlation between physical health and mental outlook. Those in good aerobic condition tend to be more self-confident, more optimistic, more determined, and to have a greater love of their jobs and professions, a higher energy level and a greater lust for life.

Your Pulse and Your Aerobic Fitness

Your pulse is a beacon of your physical fitness: when it is weak, *you* are weak; when it is strong, you are *strong*. According to Dr Laurence Moorhouse:

> 'The mortality rate for men and women with pulse rates over 92 beats per minute at rest is four times greater than for those with pulse rates less than 67 beats per minute.'

Your pulse is a wonderful index for the state of your health, fitness and emotions. It can tell you:

- how active your muscles are and how well they are functioning
- if your body's temperature is rising or falling
- how fast you are burning up energy and how efficiently you are using your oxygen supply
- how your body is faring in a battle against a marauding disease
- how your body is handling the chemical waste in your blood
- about your stress levels
- the state of your emotions and attitudes

Your pulse combines inputs from all of these and many other elements, and gives you a 'print-out' of the overall condition of your body, mind and soul.

Your resting pulse, while seated and as relaxed as you can be, gives you important information about the levels of your fitness and health. The following table gives you the standard average:

Individual	Average beats per minute
Men	72–76
Boys	80–84
Women	75–80
Girls	82–89

The reason why women and girls have, on average, slightly higher pulse rates than men is still being investigated and not yet answered!

As a general guideline, the lower your resting heart rate, the healthier you are. A resting heart rate higher than 80 beats a minute suggests poor health and fitness, and can lead to an increased risk of coronary heart disease and death in middle age. In elite athletes, the pulse rate tends to go to as low as 30–40 beats per minute (recorded by such as Miguel Indurain, the 5-times winner of the Tour de France, and Sir Steve Redgrave, the 5-times winner of rowing gold medals at the Olympics).

If your resting pulse rate is 60 beats per minute or lower, you can consider yourself very aerobically fit.

self-check – finding your pulse

Finding your pulse is easier, and becomes more easy the more fit you are. Among the best ways of finding your pulse are the following:

- Putting your hand over your heart
- Feeling the pulse in your wrist (the radial artery in your wrist, which gives you your pulse, is just inside your wrist bone at the base of your thumb joint).
- Feeling the carotid artery at the side of your neck, either just above your collarbone or below the back of your jaw – if you use this method, make sure you feel only one artery at a time, for if you feel both simultaneously you could cut off the supply of blood to your heart.
- Monitoring the temporal artery at the side of your forehead, just in front of your ear. As with the throat, press on one side only.

A good method of calculating your pulse rate per minute is to count for 6 seconds and add a zero, or count for 15 seconds and multiply by 4.

What Your Pulse Can Tell You

There are four main things you can learn about the state of your fitness when feeling your pulse:

- **The force of the pulse against your fingers.** When it is weak, you are weak; when the force is strong, you are strong. May the force be with you!
- **The expansion of your artery.** This related to the volume of blood passing through each pulse. When the volume is low, you are 'low'; when the volume increases and the artery feels more substantial, yet soft and elastic, you are fit.
- **Regularity and force of the rhythm.** When the beat is irregular and the force weak, so are you; when the rhythm is regular and the force strong, so are you.
- **Frequency.** When the frequency is high, you are slow and weak; when the frequency is low, you are strong and faster.

Jog Your Memory

Researchers at the Sork Institute for Biological Studies near San Diego in California have further confirmed the truth of the holanthropic principle: *mens sana in corpore sano*. They discovered that mice that run regularly learn more quickly than their more sedentary counterparts. Also, the running mice sprouted new brain cells in a region of the hippocampus associated with memory. The sedentary mice had no such flourishing of the dendrites! *Floreant dendritae!* May your brain cells flourish!

Recovery Heart Rate

One other major indicator of your aerobic fitness is the speed at which your pulse rate returns to normal after exercise. If you are the average untrained person, at the beginning of your training it may take you as long as 5–10 minutes for your heart rate to return to below even 100 beats per minute. As you become more fit, this 'return to below 100' will happen more rapidly. When you are super-fit, it can recover in approximately one minute!

At the same time, you can check your recovery breathing rate. Your normal resting respiratory rate ranges from between 12–16 breaths per minute. Check your own normal rate, and then compare it with your 1, 2, and 5-minute checks after exercise.

A wonderful example of confronting the Big Black Hole and learning to regulate your fitness training regime was given to me by Dr Stephen Lundin, an international level and prize-winning ergo-rower and the author of the international bestseller *Fish!*. Steve charted his progressive times over 2,500 metres, and was happily approaching record levels when he suddenly plummeted (*see* graph below). He seriously considered quitting, but after deep deliberation decided to continue. His next trial was better than he had ever done before! His *following* trial was too strenuous, and because of his astounding strength and slight misuse of himself he nearly broke his ribs with that effort! Once again, he considered the *feedback, adjusted* his approach and poise, and tried again. He remains one of the most aerobically fit people in the world.

You can recover from the 'Black Hole' of failure

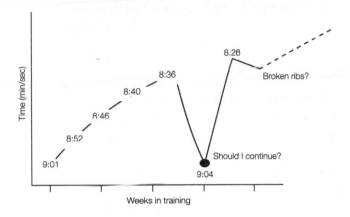

Physical Intelligence Star – Sir Ranulph Fiennes

If you wanted to look for the ideal living example of endurance and stamina, who better to look to than a man who for decades has endured near death, starvation, isolation, loneliness, severe frostbite, violent oceans and who is *still* doing it – and doing it all for charity!

I am talking, of course, of Sir Ranulph Fiennes, regularly described as the world's greatest living explorer. During the last 20 years his legendary and astonishing feats of physical and mental endurance have claimed 10 expeditionary world records, including:

- The first person ever to reach both Poles
- The first person to cross Antarctica and the Arctic Ocean

- The first person to circumnavigate earth on its Polar axis
- World record holder for unsupported Polar travel
- The longest unsupported Polar journey in history
- The first man to reach the South Pole twice
- The first man to cross the Antarctic Continent twice

Sir Ranulph has made it easy for you to select your keywords in the development of Physical Intelligence, by defining his own priority list:

Fitness	Discipline
Persistence	Enthusiasm
Creativity	Goal Setting
Determination	Planning
Patience	Ability to perform under extreme pressure

Not coincidentally, Sir Ranulph wrote a book with the same theme as our second chapter: **Mind Over Matter**.

Brain boosters

1 *I am actively working towards achieving and maintaining maximum aerobic fitness.*

2 *I am improving my physical stamina, and therefore, my mental stamina.*

3 *I am improving my mental stamina, and therefore, my physical stamina.*

4 *The force of my pulse is with me!*

chapter nine

'Age ... is a matter of feeling, not of years.'

George William Curtis

'A man is not old as long as he is seeking something.'

Jean Rostand .

> On a piece of paper, I would like you to draw an image of an 'old
> person' – one 75 years old or older. When you have drawn this,
> continue to read on.

In the more than 50 countries in 5 continents in which I have conducted this 'field experiment', the most common forms drawn to represent old people are represented below.

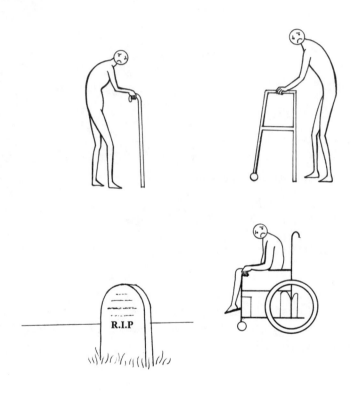

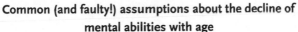

Common (and faulty!) assumptions about the decline of mental abilities with age

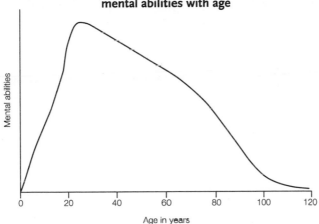

These images are horrifying *not* because they are true, but because any brain that thinks that this is what old age is going to be like, will actually create such a future for itself.

From the early chapters, you know that what the brain envisions tends to come true. Happily, observations and studies from around the world confirm that these images do *not* represent the natural progression of the human being into its senior years.

Studies on the brain have shown that the average person thinks of the decline in mental abilities with age to be dramatic (see graph above).

Similarly, they feel that the physical decline is even more dramatic (see graph p.192).

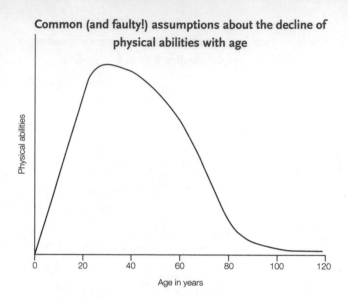

Common (and faulty!) assumptions about the decline of physical abilities with age

The fact of the matter is that both these graphs *can* be true, but only if the human beings involved *train* themselves to become worse as they get older!

Think for a moment about anybody you know who is over 75, and who does not fit the normal profile of an elderly person. Then make a list of their characteristics.

Now check the characteristics of those people who have been found by studies to contradict the popular misconception. The words used to describe them are as follows:

Patriarchs   Oracles   Veterans

Elders

Sages   All-seeing   Troisieme age

Venerable   Matriarchs   The Revered

Gurus

Oral historians   O Senseis   Les Vieux

Paterfamilias

These characteristics describe the natural (not 'normal') progression of fully-integrated Physically Intelligent beings through all the years of life.

The *real* graphs of human mentally and physically integrated development are as follows.

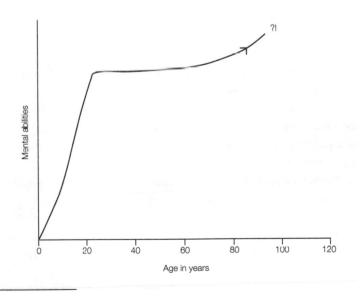

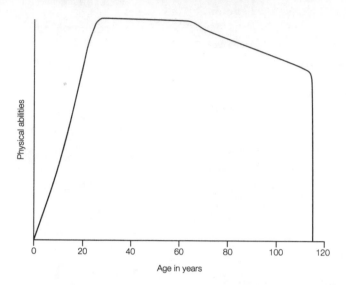

We are now finding that what used to be considered physically normal behaviours and capacities for a 30-year old, now apply to 60–70-year olds! And even further on into the decades, 70-year olds are climbing five mountains in a month to celebrate their eighth decade, 90-year olds (plus!) are swimming 100-metre dashes at rates close to that of the Olympic champions of a mere 80 years ago, and all the physical boundaries are being pushed back day by day by day.

Envision your physical progression through life to be one of increasing vigour and energy, and it can become so.

Nurture all the aspects of your Physical Intelligence covered in the previous eight chapters and the words that will describe you in your senior years will be those you have just read on page 193; and the images that will describe you and your friends will *not* be those on page 190, they will be these:

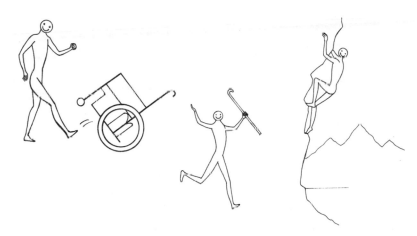

Physical Intelligence Star – Sir Mick Jagger

Looking at him with the same Sherlock Holmesian objectivity you used to investigate a good diet and appropriate attitude to drugs, you will quickly come to realize that Sir Mick is a phenomenal example of manifest Physical Intelligence, as well as being one of the ground-breakers in smashing inappropriate global beliefs about physical ageing. Many have assumed that his life was one of pure dissipation, but nothing could be further from the truth – if it had been he would not have been able to accomplish what he has.

Consider that in an average performance, Mick 'runs' about a half marathon! Not only does he do this, he does it while crouching, leaping and singing at full volume, often, in his longer concerts, approaching a *full* marathon!

In addition to this, he has full rehearsals, which are often longer than the concerts themselves, as well as a punishing schedule of travel. On 17-city tours he is approaching the musical and physical equivalent of Lance Armstrong's Tour de France.

And he does it at the age of 60! With no signs of slowing down ...

There are also many more 'strings to his guitar' and aspects of his personality and intelligences than many people know about.

For example, Mick used his considerable mental energies to overcome shyness, and his considerable intellect to gain entrance to the prestigious London School of Economics where he studied Business. Mick is a lot more rational and reasonable than many people have given him credit for, and although a risk taker, he lives by his own dictum, 'It is alright letting yourself go, as long as you can get yourself back!'

Like other Physical Intelligence stars, Mick is also a positive and creative thinker. His skinny, lanky frame and rubbery lips made him the exact opposite of the poster-boy pop stars of the time, so Mick used his creativity and business skills to turn these 'disadvantages' into unique qualities and saleable commodities. Again disproving the current beliefs about declining creativity with age, Mick has turned his considerable skills to acting, writing and film production, while continuing to write music and songs.

Mick keeps himself fit by long-distance running and by paying very close attention to his healthy diet. He and Tina Turner are living proof that the attitudes about the latter stages of the 'ages of man and woman' are in for a real shake out!

Brain boosters

1 *I am young in heart; young in mind.*
2 *As I progress through life, I am continuing to develop and hone my physical and mental skills.*
3 *I am developing a mental vision of age as healthy, robust, energetic, flexible, productive, happy and strong.*

physical plus – applying your physical intelligence to multiplying your other multiple intelligences

chapter ten

As you are about to become a graduate of *The Power of Physical Intelligence*, and as you realize more of the benefits of an holanthropic approach to your life, you have become increasingly aware of how every aspect of your Physical Intelligence relates to and enhances every other aspect.

Happily, this compound interest formula can be multiplied even further to your advantage.

With the full power of your Physical Intelligence beginning to express itself, you can use it to enhance the power of your other Multiple Intelligences, and use *their* power to yet further enhance the power of your own Physical Intelligence.

social intelligence

What, traditionally, are the characteristics of the stars and leaders to whom everyone looks up?

If you think about it you will realize that it is their energy, their power, their flexibility – both mental and physical – their radiance, their strength, their confidence and their poise.

These characteristics also sum up the characteristics of the Super-Physically Intelligent individual. As you continue to develop your Physical Intelligence, your Social Intelligence and therefore your popularity and success with others will continue to rise.

You can also use social opportunities for physical activity with others, including dancing, travelling, and all sports and games activities, to give you an ideal opportunity for enhancing your physical skills and intelligence. Your Physical and Social Intelligences are particularly close and mutually enhancing team members!

personal intelligence

Your Personal Intelligence is your ability to be your own best friend; to get along with yourself, and to be happy and content with and within yourself. When you are physically healthy, your body and mind will constantly be cleansed, all your major body systems will be in harmony with each other, and your internal and external rhythms will be healthy and strong. As such, you will automatically be stable and more confident.

You will look good, feel good and be an even more enjoyable person to spend time with. Including with yourself. You can also use your Personal Intelligence to improve your Physical Intelligence.

One of the greatest causes of physical ill health is, as you know, negative stress. One of the worst forms of negative stress is not liking yourself; being ill at ease with yourself.

The minute your Personal Intelligence begins to rise, stress levels are automatically reduced, your immune system is strengthened, your body and senses open up, and overall physical health and energy results.

sensual intelligence

Your senses are your vanguard – your reconnaissance scouts.

As we have already seen, your senses are in every sense Super-Senses, and are a significant part of your overall Physical Intelligence. Leonardo da Vinci considered Sensual Intelligence to be the most important intelligence of all.

Your senses are the ultimately sophisticated sensors with which your brain explores its Universe. Developing this intelligence will initiate the wonderfully synergetic spiral in which, with each sense being increasingly developed, your health and overall Physical Intelligence will rise. Similarly, as your overall health and Physical Intelligence rise, so will your Sensual Intelligence.

spatial intelligence

Spatial Intelligence involves your ability to perceive and negotiate three-dimensional space. One of the most common ways of doing this is with our bodies. Ultimate expressions of Spatial Intelligence include: dance, sport, and any form of outdoor physical activity. The more you develop your Physical Intelligence in these areas, especially with games such as ball games, the more you will simultaneously be developing your Spatial Intelligence. The more you develop your Physical Intelligence in such activities, the more you will be developing your Spatial Intelligence. Once again, a synergetic co-operation between your Multiple Intelligences!

creative intelligence

Your Creative Intelligence is one of your most explosive abilities. It involves the ability of your brain to think fast, to imagine on vast scales, to think originally and to forge new associations between things.

And what does all this?

Your brain! The most developed evolutionary organ, and the crowning glory of your physical being. If it is 'in shape', its thinking powers will similarly be 'in shape'. This is another excellent example of *mens sana in corpore sano*: healthy mind–healthy body, healthy body–healthy mind.

The Greeks practised it. The Romans practised it. The studies confirm it. Common sense confirms it.

You and I should practise it too!

Summary advice

In order for you to develop the healthiest mind in the healthiest body, the following action steps are highly recommended:

1 Do aerobic training for at least 20 minutes, 4 times a week.
2 In conjunction with your aerobic training, increase your flexibility.
3 In conjunction with aerobics and flexibility, develop the strength of your entire muscular system.
4 Develop and improve your poise.
5 Create a mastermind group of health advisers as you would if you were a professional athlete (remember just how priceless your own body is). This group might include specialists, doctors, coaches, Alexander technique teachers, and nutritional experts.
6 Incorporate regular rest periods in your daily, weekly, monthly, yearly and overall life – they will give your life more quality and help it be longer.
7 Find time to play. Play is one of the best forms of all-round exercise, especially when you have the opportunity to play with children – they will make a hard work-out in the gym appear like a rest period!
8 Establish and monitor a basic healthy diet.

9   Enjoy regular romantic and/or sexual activity.

10 Give your brain regular doses of its four basic Brain Foods: oxygen, good nutrition, continued learning, and affection and love.

11 Know yourself better. Monitor and measure your physical variables, and chart the various forms of your athletic progress.

12 Do a creative Mind Map on your current physical levels and your future goals. Immediately put these goals into action. Remember, you are in the process ...

Physical Intelligence Star – Ellen MacArthur

One of the most incredible examples of Physical Intelligence ever, demonstrating persistence, flexibility, inner personal strength, communication skills, and sheer bloody-mindedness and guts, was Ellen MacArthur's single-handed circumnavigation of the globe.

Magellan would have been proud of her!

To add to the stature of her incredible performance, Ellen was also the youngest competitor ever to finish the Round the World Yacht Race, and only the second person in history to sail around the world solo in under 100 days.

Even more extraordinary was that this young woman was a tiny (5ft 2in), 24-year old from Derbyshire, and that she was competing alone against the best and much bigger and stronger male sailors in the world. Even *more* extraordinary was that she became easily the fastest woman to complete the single-handed non-stop race and came second overall!

To make all of this even more riveting, the entire event was filmed, so millions of people around the world saw a tiny lone figure being assaulted by 50-foot waves, frozen, blasted by relentless sun, climbing up and fixing broken masts in howling gales and generally being battered and bruised by the elements.

Throughout the ordeal, Ellen kept a video log which showed her sometimes exultant, sometimes in despair. But even in the most terrifying and depressing moments, her indomitable will won through, her mind driving her body through Herculean tasks that even our other Physical Intelligence stars might find daunting.

She was named 'World Sailor of the Year' by both the British and International Sailing Federation in 2001. To millions of people around the world she was the World Sports Personality of the Year.

Ellen's mind-over-matter approach was summed up in an article in the *Daily Telegraph* under the title 'Brain Power':

'There are sporting heroes to treasure, those who by achievement and behaviour are perfect role models. Ellen MacArthur and Paula Radcliffe come to mind.'

Something MacArthur said should serve as the mantra for all athletes who want to reach the top in any sport:

'In the final analysis, what matters most are not muscles but what goes on in the brain.'

Brain boosters

1   *I am using the multiple skills of my Social Intelligence to develop my Physical Intelligence.*

2   *I am using the multiple skills of my Spatial Intelligence to develop my Physical Intelligence.*

3   *I am using the multiple skills of my Personal Intelligence to develop my Physical Intelligence.*

4   *I am using the multiple skills of my Sensual Intelligence to develop my Physical Intelligence.*

5   *I am using the multiple skills of my Sexual Intelligence to develop my Physical Intelligence.*

If you want to learn more about Physical Intelligence, and to take part in games, quizzes and discussions around all of the subjects covered here, why don't you visit

www.buzancentres.com

or contact Tony at the Buzan Centre:

HEADQUARTERS – U.K.
The Buzan Centres Ltd
54 Parkstone Road
Poole, Dorset BH15 2PG
Tel: +44 (0)1202 674676
Fax: +44 (0)1202 674776

HEADQUARTERS – U.S.A.
A Buzan Centre of Palm Beach Inc.
PO Box 4
Palm Beach
FL 33480
Tel: +1 561 881 0188
Tel: 866 896 1024 (U.S.A. Toll-Free)

or e-mail: buzan@buzancentres.com

index

Make
www.thorsonselement.com
your online sanctuary